The End of the Gold

NEW ZEALAND PLAYSCRIPTS

GENERAL EDITOR: JOHN THOMSON

Glide Time by Roger Hall
Middle Age Spread by Roger Hall
Awatea by Bruce Mason
The Pohutukawa Tree by Bruce Mason
The Two Tigers by Brian McNeill
State of the Play by Roger Hall
Jack Winter's Dream by James K Baxter
Foreskin's Lament by Greg McGee
Bruce Mason Solo (hardcover)
Blood of the Lamb by Bruce Mason
Fifty-Fifty by Roger Hall
Hot Water by Roger Hall
Outside In by Hilary Beaton
The End of the Golden Weather by Bruce Mason
Out in the Cold by Greg McGee
Tooth and Claw by Greg McGee
Shuriken by Vincent O'Sullivan
Objection Overruled by Carolyn Burns
Wednesday to Come by Renée
Driftwood by Rachel McAlpine
Pass It On by Renée
Coaltown Blues by Mervyn Thompson
The Healing Arch by Bruce Mason
Squatter by Stuart Hoar
The Share Club by Roger Hall
A Red Mole Sketchbook by Alan Brunton
Three Radio Plays
Jones & Jones by Vincent O'Sullivan
The Land of the Moa by George Leitch
Billy by Vincent O'Sullivan
Jeannie Once by Renée
Broken Arse by Bruce Stewart
Daughters of Heaven by Michelanne Forster
Joyful and Triumphant by Robert Lord
Lovelock's Dream Run by David Geary
Verbatim by William Brandt
Nga Tangata Toa by Hone Kouka
Eugenia by Lorae Parry
Ta Matou Mangai / Our Own Voice edited by Hone Kouka

The End of the Golden Weather

A voyage into a
New Zealand childhood
by Bruce Mason

Victoria University Press

VICTORIA UNIVERSITY PRESS
Victoria University of Wellington
PO Box 600 Wellington
http://www.vup.vuw.ac.nz

ISBN 0 86473 272 4

First published in 1962
This edition revised and reset in 1970
Reprinted 1974, 1981, 1994, 1998

Cover design by Graham Percy

Printed by South Wind Production (Singapore) Pte Ltd

CONTENTS

Sunday at Te Parenga
page 35

The night of the riots
page 45

Christmas at Te Parenga
page 53

The made man
page 65

To B.C.
Deer stalker, friend

Note to the second edition

About a year ago, I was invited by the New Zealand Broadcasting Corporation to prepare a television programme to celebrate the 500th performance of *The End of the Golden Weather;* it reached the screen in another form, and was shown on all channels in the *Looking at New Zealand* series on Sunday, 14 September, 1969, directed by John Barningham and produced by Bute Hewes. My original TV script gives a fuller account of the experience, and I offer it here, exactly as it was submitted, omitting only technical terms of the TV trade.

AUTHOR *can be seen advancing to table and chair; unseen applause. Bow.*

AUTHOR. 'I invite you to join me, in a voyage into the past, to that territory of the heart we call childhood. . . .'

Camera recedes, showing AUTHOR *mumbling on a TV screen; voice fades to murmur, as he says:*

'Consider, if you will, Te Parenga. . . .'

He drones on, behind the montage of press clippings, reviews, the published text, the two record covers. Camera now reveals a studio, the AUTHOR *and* INTERVIEWER, *facing each other.*

TITLES: *The Golden Weather Odyssey, or Fleecings from the Golden Weather, by Bruce Mason.*

INTERVIEWER. *The End of the Golden Weather.* How many times now?

7

AUTHOR. I lost count after 500.

INTERVIEWER. Almost a way of life.

AUTHOR. Almost.

INTERVIEWER. You must have asked yourself: will it ever end?

AUTHOR. I still do it: between thirty and fifty performances every year.

INTERVIEWER. And you never tire of it?

AUTHOR. Never. You see I've no aids at all. Table, chair, voice, gesture. Nothing else. So it has to be re-created on the spot, every time. Every audience is different; every audience a new challenge.

INTERVIEWER. And you've taken it everywhere.

AUTHOR. You name it: I've played it.

INTERVIEWER. Blenheim.

AUTHOR. No.

INTERVIEWER. Alexandra.

AUTHOR. No. You've picked the only two. But everywhere else, of any size. Every city, town, village, hamlet, petrol-station, it sometimes seems.

INTERVIEWER. How did it all begin?

AUTHOR. Well, in 1959, I'd come to the end of a road. I'd written a few plays, assembled a mountain of criticism, done some producing. I'd had a crack at all the arts and trades of theatre. But it hadn't got me anywhere.

INTERVIEWER. Where did you want to get?

AUTHOR. I just wanted to feel that I had a calling for theatre and that this calling would at length be recognised, so that I could give my life and best energies to it. But you can't work in a vacuum. A man won't write symphonies, if there's no orchestra to play them. There was no solid theatrical framework here, no ladder to climb so that, feet on the the first rung, you could go upwards to the second. You created no *mana,* no reputation or authority to justify your work. In fact, to most people, it wasn't work at all, just pretentious frivolity.

INTERVIEWER. What about the New Zealand Players?

AUTHOR. A flash in the pan, alas, though a flash that lasted for seven years.

INTERVIEWER. But didn't you write for them?

AUTHOR. Yes. Sketches and pieces for their Schools' Quartets and one full-length play, which has become my best-known: *The Pohutukawa Tree*. But at no stage could I consider that this was opening up a career. It was always and only, a spare-time job. Hence the desperation.

INTERVIEWER. And? So?

AUTHOR. Well, I'm a Kiwi, born and bred. We're at our best in a corner: good improvisers, bad experts, as an American critic once said of us. No theatrical framework? Right, then, I would create my own. Touring a play is expensive? Then cut to the minimum, table and chair. Scenery is costly to make and cumbersome to cart around? Do it all with words: appeal directly to the audience's imagination. Casts are expensive? Be your own. Do all forty parts. Play any-where, in any circumstances, to any audience.

INTERVIEWER. You take my breath away.

AUTHOR. I almost took my own away.

INTERVIEWER. But how much experience did you have for this?

AUTHOR. Very little; none, of solo theatre.

INTERVIEWER. Aren't I right in saying that there are only about six people in the entire English-speaking world who have the—

AUTHOR. Effrontery is the word that eludes you.

INTERVIEWER. All right, effrontery, to dare to hold an audience on their speaking voice alone?

AUTHOR. Yes, and I can name them. Hal Holbrook, who does Mark Twain. Joyce Grenfell, though she sings also, Sir John Gielgud with his Shakespeare recital, *The Ages of Man*, Orson Welles from time to time, with this and that, Micheal McLiammoir with *The Importance of Being Oscar* (*Wilde*), Emlyn Williams, with his Dickens and Dylan Thomas evenings. . . .

INTERVIEWER. Yes, he visited New Zealand in 1958, with both programmes.

AUTHOR. I went to see them, and saw what could be done. I wrote to Mr Williams, and asked if I could meet him and tell him what I had in mind.

INTERVIEWER. What did he say?

9

AUTHOR. I think he was stupefied by my audacity. He said something like this. That he had been thirty years in the professional theatre, both as an actor and as a playwright. His *Night Must Fall* and *The Corn is Green* had both had lengthy runs on the stage, in England and America, both had been made into successful films, with top stars. Yet when in 1950, he asked his management, H. M. Tennent Ltd., the most prosperous in London, to arrange and present a solo evening of Dickens readings for him, they were dubious almost to hostility; finally, at his insistence, they agreed to give him a Sunday-night try-out in Cambridge. "And remember," he said to me, "I wasn't proposing to stand on my own reputation alone; I stood on Dickens' shoulders, and later, on Dylan Thomas'. Yet here, little you, at the backyard of the world, dare to assume that you can not only hold an audience oy yourself, but you write your own script as well! Weᴊ, there's nothing to do but wish you luck."

INTERVIEWER. Were you dashed by this?

AUTHOR. A bit, but there was nothing to do but try. I had a few advantages, negative ones, but important. I didn't have to impress an agent or management; we have neither. I took no financial or professional risk. If I wanted to do it, there was no one to say no. Nor, when one begins, is there anyone to say yes. You just have to go over the top, into No Man's Land. So I got my script in order—it all fell together quite neatly, once I had made my decision—and first tottered onto the fit-up stage of the old New Zealand Players Workshop, mouth dry, knees knocking, in August, 1959.

INTERVIEWER. How did it go?

AUTHOR. It was a disaster. I had a mild throat infection, exacerbated by nerves; I collapsed in hoarse shrieks, my lips stuck together, about a third from the end: Stafford Byrne, then Artistic Director of the New Zealand Players, bounded out of the audience and made a chivalrous, gallant speech. I rallied and just scraped home. One of the reviews next day was excoriating, dwelling gleefully on all the mishaps, calling it pretentious piffle, ending crushingly, "New Zealand cannot yet, it seems, produce an Emlyn Williams."

INTERVIEWER. Why should it?

AUTHOR. Why, indeed? I wasn't out to imitate anybody, only to offer myself, to the best of my skill. So I picked myself up, and went on, and gave a dozen or so performances round the town in the next few weeks. Then, early in 1960, the CAS in Otago—

INTERVIEWER. CAS? Explain.

AUTHOR. The Community Arts Service of the Regional Councils for Adult Education. They hardly exist now, except for a little music, but they performed an invaluable service for isolated communities before television. They had opera, theatre, ballet or music, three or four times a year; active local committees engaged a group or a person, and rallied the community to prepare halls and cut sandwiches; a CAS visit was a real communal work-out. Well, the CAS in Otago, Canterbury and Wellington offered me a three-month tour of their provinces. I found it invaluable. I'd done some acting for amateur groups, and a good deal on radio, but no more than many of my age and less than some. New Zealand did not then offer any professional training for an actor, so I had to learn mine on the job which, all said and done, is the best way. I had to develop a light and not very flexible baritone into an instrument which would not only be adequate for my forty-odd characters, but reach to the back of the vast echoing barns I found myself in; having no properties, not a stick on stage, I had to become skilful in mime, or the show wouldn't work. It was an unrivalled training, for which I shall always be grateful.

INTERVIEWER. And which, from what you say, you wouldn't get now.

AUTHOR. No, I don't think so. The touring circuit has collapsed, everywhere.

INTERVIEWER. So all this began a circuit that took you eventually to the Edinburgh Festival?

AUTHOR. Yes, in 1963.

INTERVIEWER. What did the Scots make of something so essentially New Zealand?

AUTHOR. They laughed in different places, at different things. They split their Scottish sides at my description of a

11

gargantuan Christmas dinner at 88 degrees in the shade; here there was silence at this, its incongruity unnoticed. Here audiences laughed at what was familiar; there at what was exotic.

INTERVIEWER. And what is the purpose of *Golden Weather?* What made you do it? Pick this particular form and scene?

AUTHOR. It all began by accident, as such things tend to. I had given a series of radio talks about my interest in theatre, which began when I was very young. This brought back into my mind a host of people I had forgotten: there, suddenly, was Part I of *Golden Weather.*

INTERVIEWER. I believe the title was even quoted in Parliament a couple of years ago. Referring to our economic situation— devaluation was the nut being cracked—a Labour member noted that "Yes, Mr Speaker: this is the end of the golden weather, but *not* by Bruce Mason."

AUTHOR. Flattering, but the title is the one thing in the piece which isn't original. It's from Thomas Wolfe, the American author of *The Web and the Rock* and *Look Homeward, Angel,* which I had devoured when I was young. I remembered that the narrator in *The Web and the Rock* had spoken of a novel that he wanted to write, but never did. I can recall the passage, as I should: it appears on every programme.

INTERVIEWER. Shoot.

AUTHOR. 'The subject he chose for his first effort was a boy's vision of life over a ten-month period, between his twelfth and thirteenth year and the title was *The End of The Golden Weather.* By this title, he meant to describe that change in the *colour* of life which every child has known— the change from the enchanted light and weather of his soul, the full golden light, the magic green and gold in which he sees the earth in childhood. . . .'

INTERVIEWER. Bit lush, isn't it?

AUTHOR. Yes, a bit. But it's heady stuff when you're young.

INTERVIEWER. Sorry: I interrupted.

AUTHOR. 'He prepared to tell how at this period in a child's life, this strange and magic light—this *golden weather*— begins to change and, for the first time, some of the troubling weathers of a man's soul are revealed to him; and how, for the first time, he becomes aware of the thousand changing visages of time, touched with confusion and bewilderment, menaced by terrible depths and enigmas of experience he has never known before. He wanted to tell the story of this year exactly as he had remembered it, with all the things and people he had known that year.'

INTERVIEWER. And that's what you did?

AUTHOR. To the letter. Once I had read that, all the things and people came pounding back.

INTERVIEWER. And how did the people take it?

AUTHOR. What people?

INTERVIEWER. The people you had known.

AUTHOR. Well, I didn't put them down exactly as I had known them. Except for my parents, brother and sister.

INTERVIEWER. What did they think?

AUTHOR. My parents took it very well. They came to one of my Wellington performances. I was a bit nervy about them being there. My father came into my dressing room and said "Well my boy; I don't think I was as nice as all that!"

INTERVIEWER. And your mother?

AUTHOR. There's a lot in the piece, especially in *Christmas at Te Parenga*, about food. All my mother said afterwards was "Well, dear: I'm very relieved to know that I had such a well-stocked house!" My sister, who I described in one passage as a "frilly, pink, smiling sausage" was not all that charmed, but forgave me, and my brother has lived in South Africa since 1947, so he has never seen it. But he's heard it on records and read the book: no complaint.

INTERVIEWER. But Te Parenga . . . that's what you call your beach, isn't it, Te Parenga?

AUTHOR. Yes.

INTERVIEWER. What's it mean?

AUTHOR. I chose it for euphony, without knowing what it means, or even if it had a meaning. However, it does: it means 'the river bank,' not quite what I had in mind, though near enough to the sloping terrace rising from the beach that I describe.

INTERVIEWER. What's its real name?

AUTHOR. Te Parenga.

INTERVIEWER. Oh, come. You know what I mean.

AUTHOR. Yes, I know exactly what you mean, but its real name is still Te Parenga. I mention in it several things that you will find on or see from a particular Auckland beach, but others I have changed as it suited me, so that it ceases to be that beach and becomes the one I call Te Parenga. The people, too. You start perhaps with a living model, but as you work on him, he changes and, in a sense, takes you over.

Change of dimension: AUTHOR *in performance, describing* SERGEANT ROBINSON.

'Promptly at eleven, Sergeant Robinson appears on the beach. He has been Te Parenga's sergeant of police for over thirty years. Small, fierce-eyed, round and gnarled as a nut, he strides along with a nuggety grandeur, clean white Sunday shirt blazing, no tie, helmet just the merest trifle askew to show that he is not on duty, striped braces straining like hawsers over his shoulders, pausing to chat with his friends, regally acknowledging salvoes of greetings from all over the beach. . .'

Recede to INTERVIEWER.

INTERVIEWER. That seems harmless enough.

AUTHOR. I thought so too, until there was an article in the local paper—

INTERVIEWER. What local paper?

AUTHOR. The paper local to the place that has assumed it is Te Parenga, saying that my performance at the Auckland Festival of 1965 would allow residents to catch up with or meet again old friends like Miss This and Sergeant That; I had to write a letter to the paper stating that, whatever material I might have started with, the finished article bore no resemblance to the original.

INTERVIEWER. How did they take it?

AUTHOR. There was a headline in the next issue, saying that I disclaimed all responsibility for my characters; that they bore no resemblance whatever to people either living or dead. And that's not quite true, either. It's just that when you work from living material, people all too readily assume that the finished product is a kind of piracy or pillage, looted from life. It can never be so. I deliberately made my sergeant a small nuggety man, because the man I remember was enormous. But the 'Te Parenga' audiences blew him up like a barrage balloon into the policeman they remembered. I was accused of offence to a lady I had never met, nor even heard of before, and there was one worse one—

INTERVIEWER. Tell.

AUTHOR. Well, Golden Weather is divided into two parts, the first given over mostly to creating the landscape and introducing the characters, engaged in simple domestic rituals: between two lightish pieces, there is a serious one about the depression, that strange and alarming period when the land of milk and honey turned to bread and dripping. The second half is called *The Made Man,* with a central character I call Firpo, after a famous South American boxer of the twenties, who took from Jack Dempsey the world heavyweight title. Simple-minded, my Firpo is the butt of the district, and thinks he is a great athlete. He is egged on to this not only by the young louts of the district, the kind of irresponsible youths you will find anywhere, prepared to destroy a man for laughs, or as we say now, kicks, but also by the young narrator, who sees in the man a symbolic importance and mystery, revealed in this speech. . . .

Author as FIRPO.

'Firpo's the name. You know that, don't you? Well, Firpo can do anything at all, see, anything you like to name. But what do they do to Firpo, eh? Yeh: what do they do? They shut him up, they hide him away from the sun, they give him another name. But it's Firpo, Firpo, always Firpo! The time's coming, ohohoho yes, it's not far away! when Firpo will have his day and what will he be then?

A made man. Did you hear me, boy? Shall I say it again?
A made man. Made Man! Made man! Made man! . . .'

AUTHOR. Well, the boy gets excited at this: sees in Firpo a chance
to make him the chief character in his own fiction, as it
were, make him over, like God.

INTERVIEWER. The terrible depths? The enigmas of experience?

AUTHOR. Well, as near as I can get to them. And of course,
Firpo comes to ruin; he is shut away for good.

INTERVIEWER. Moral: don't make living people characters in
your own fiction.

AUTHOR. That, and more. Don't ask them to act out any fiction
but their own. Most people don't: they're too keen on
themselves, anyway. But Firpo was vulnerable, without the
brains or the insight to resist, so he's doomed.

INTERVIEWER. So that's what *Golden Weather* is about?

AUTHOR. Yes, in the end; that *is* the end of the golden weather.
I thought I was proclaiming a truth, by setting it down as
fiction. But you just listen to this.

A middle-aged man, knocks at an imaginary door.

MAN. Mr Mason?

AUTHOR. Yes.

MAN. About Firpo.

AUTHOR. Well?

MAN. I've had a hideous evening.

AUTHOR. Why?

MAN. Because I certified that man.

AUTHOR. You're a doctor?

MAN. Yes. His name was—

AUTHOR. Please don't tell me. I don't want to know. Anyway,
you couldn't have.

MAN. Certified? I tell you—

AUTHOR. He doesn't exist. At least, not in your world, to be
certified.

MAN. That was him! I heard his voice, saw him standing there,
right in front of me, just as he was. Took me back thirty
years.

AUTHOR. I never knew anyone called Firpo. I heard the name

when I was a boy, but I was never sure whom it fitted. I do remember a couple of old weirdies on the beach, but I never spoke a word to either, in my life.

MAN. You could have his family on to you.

AUTHOR. He's fiction. Based on memory, on hints and suggestions from here and there. Fiction.

MAN. There should be a law about it. Hurting people's feelings.

AUTHOR. There is. Libel. But there's been no libel.

MAN. You think I'd go about, exposing my patients? What's to stop me getting on my hind legs and shooting my mouth off about my interesting cases?

AUTHOR. The will, perhaps. And the time. And possibly, the gift?

MAN. Don't you worry. I could get a big crowd. Spread the word, spread the dirt: they'd come running.

AUTHOR. No they wouldn't. Art isn't a case history. Literature isn't life.

MAN. To hell with literature; you've got me all stirred up; haven't thought of that poor old coot since 1936—

AUTHOR. Why 1936?

MAN. He hanged himself. In the asylum. With his belt.

AUTHOR. Then I don't see that I've hurt anyone.

MAN, *fading:* There ought to be a law. Bloody literature, stirring us all up. . . .

INTERVIEWER.

INTERVIEWER. Small country.

AUTHOR. And terrified of being exposed.

INTERVIEWER. I suppose the best-known single episode of *Golden Weather* is the one about the riots.

AUTHOR. Yes, it was printed separately, for schools. I wonder if it made more sense read, than in performance.

INTERVIEWER. Explain.

AUTHOR. I showed them a glimpse of the land of milk and honey, turning without warning, into bread and dripping. It seemed inexplicable; because of events on the other side of the world. And when I've done it for schools, they just didn't believe it. I showed them Sergeant Robinson, everyone's friend, turning in a flash to their enemy. All relationships changed overnight. It was a knife coming down, cutting into past and future. It fell into my schools performances with a damp plop.

INTERVIEWER. I suppose they've never known bread and dripping. But your older audiences must have.

AUTHOR. They used to come round afterwards, to talk about it.

INTERVIEWER. What I did in the Great Depression?

AUTHOR. No, not quite. Not in any boastful way. Quiet and painful memories, mostly. I could have filled a book with what I heard. Here's one: typical enough.

MIDDLE-AGED MAN.

MAN. Yeh: well I was eighteen in 1932. Southland lad. Nothing to do when I left school, no jobs. We'd gather every morning, hundreds of us, outside the Labour Office, and kick up merry hell. Well, they had to do something, so one day a joker came out, got us all into a group and told us we were going up the river valleys, high in the back country, to sluice for gold.

Took us a day and a half to get there, in a long line of trucks; jammed in, sitting up straight, with an older joker on each truck, to keep us in order. We sang all the way up, clean songs first, then, when we ran out of these, dirty songs. God knows what we had to sing about. Camp was tents, leaky old jobs from the First World War, sleeping ten apiece. Food was soup, twice a day. Out every morning by 7 o'clock, down to the river. All day long, on your knees, or up to your pills in freezing water, sluicing away for gold that was cut right out of it, a hundred years back. Once in a while, one of us would find a speck, just a thread in a piece of quartz, break it down with a hammer, scrape up a few grains, a little dust. And we'd hold these grains in our hands as if we were millionaires, give it to the overseer feller, get a receipt; he'd send it to Dunedin. What you found, you got current value for: four quid an ounce. No one got an ounce, not in the whole six months we were there. Yeh: that's what we did for six solid months, in freezing cold water. Sluice, sluice, sluice: find anything, back to Dunedin with it, then they locked it in a vault. Jokers looking after us had a tough job; always fights at night, anything, anything, stop us going cuckoo. Whole world seemed mad; eighteen-year-old-kids, best time of their lives should be, sluicing away for gold that wasn't there, freezing to death; find a grain, take it off you, lock it in a vault. . . .

AUTHOR. I thought, when I first started to perform *Golden Weather,* that *I* had something to offer; that, in my own way, I was showing my countrymen themselves. What was really happening—though I didn't know it at first—was that I was learning from them; that they were revealing the country to me. I could have written another *Golden Weather* from the tours. If the people were warm, the towns were dreary in the extreme. I remember writing a bitchy little poem, as I came into a graceless dump in the north, beginning: "The town is as casual as dust. . . ." But, going everywhere, into every corner, I came to know it as few have had the chance to. The CAS circuit, night after night, once for 100 nights on end, six nights a week, every night in a different town, different bed, different people; one night you had your own bathroom, next night you were in the nursery, sharing with little Jimmy. But the meal was always the same: roast mutton, roast potatoes and pumpkin. I must have eaten half a ton of pumpkin in the first five years. I hope it doesn't seem churlish, but I got so that I hoped I never saw pumpkin again. . . .

INTERVIEWER. How did you find country people?

AUTHOR. As audiences?

INTERVIEWER. Yes.

AUTHOR. More responsive and alert than city ones. They seemed genuinely grateful that you'd come their way. Not always, though, too grateful that you were staying in their house. . . .

MAN *sitting in front of fire, reading newspaper. Wife appears through door, leading* AUTHOR.

WIFE, *approaching Man:* George, dear. This is Mr Mason.

MAN *turns slowly in chair, looks* AUTHOR *up and down, turns back to paper.*

MAN. And what kind of useless bugger are you?

Pause. WIFE *gasps.*

AUTHOR. I'll leave that to you. After you've seen the show.
MAN. What bloody show?
WIFE, *unhappily:* You know perfectly well, George. I've told you, several times.
MAN. Singing, Dancing, Showing off. Bloody exhibitionism. Crap. Crap!
WIFE, *anguished:* Oh, George! Mr Mason is our guest.
MAN. What's he done, to be our guest?
WIFE, *quietly:* I invited him. That makes him our guest.
MAN. I'll bet. She's the culture queen round here. Brahms in X sharp minor. Well, what do you do for a crust? Sing? Dance? Play the fool?
AUTHOR. No, I just talk.
MAN. For how long?
AUTHOR. Two hours.
MAN. Christ!
AUTHOR. There's a fifteen minute interval.
MAN. And you'd need it, by God! What do you talk about?
AUTHOR. Come and see.
MAN. I'm damned if I'm coming to see high-falutin crap!
WIFE. George: how do you know if you don't go?
MAN, *curiously:* You get paid, for shooting your mouth off?
AUTHOR. I get a fee.
MAN. How much?
AUTHOR. On this tour, I get twelve guineas a night. Less tax.
MAN. Jesus wept. Twelve guineas a night? Easy money, eh boy? You know what I did today? Milked 140 cows before breakfast. Up at four. And now here comes a useless coot who talks two bloody hours and gets paid for it. Something cockeyed, somewhere.

WIFE *in tears.*

Oh, boy. Here we go again.

WIFE. Why can't you be nicer to our guests?

MAN. He's no guest of mine.

Glum pause.

Do you drink? Like a shot?

AUTHOR. Yes, I do, but not before a show.

MAN, *very sarcastic:* Oh, excuse me! Have to save our golden voice, do we?

WIFE, *anguished:* George!

MAN *looks at her, picks up his paper, retreats behind it.* WIFE *beckons.* AUTHOR *to follow her.*

WIFE. He's not always like this. Works too hard. Hoped the two boys would help him, but they've gone off to the city; can't stand farm life, too lonely for the young nowadays. Works harder now than when we were married. Not as fit as he was. . . .

INTERVIEWER. That was some reception. How did it end?

AUTHOR. Like this. Watch.

WIFE, AUTHOR *returning after performance.*

WIFE, *warmly:* Oh, I did enjoy it! Goodness me: brought back things I'd forgotten for years! You know that bit where, if you get to the telegraph pole before the bus, a wish will come true?

AUTHOR. Yes.

WIFE. I did that. I thought I was the only one. I did that, just the same . . . George! Not here. Must have gone to bed. . . . No, the truck's not here. Must have gone to see his cobbers. . . .

MAN *comes in. He goes up to* AUTHOR *and looks at him curiously.*

WIFE. You been out, George?

21

MAN, *still looking at* AUTHOR: Yes. Went out.

WIFE. Where?

MAN. I sat at the back.

WIFE. George! You went to the show!

MAN, *flatly:* Yes, I went. *To* AUTHOR, *challengingly:* You answer a question?

AUTHOR. I'll try.

MAN. Was that literature?

AUTHOR. It's nice of you to ask, but it's not for me to say. If you thought so, I'm very pleased.

MAN. Was it culture, then?

AUTHOR. Again: if you thought so.

MAN, *expansively:* I don't give a stuff if it was or not. That spoke to me. Opened up my life, things I'd forgotten. That was me, there. I was on that beach; I was at that Christmas party. I had an Uncle Jim, just like that noisy bastard. Why didn't you tell me it was like that?

AUTHOR. You hardly gave me the chance.

MAN. Bloody rude, wasn't I?

WIFE. Yes, George: you were!

MAN. I was asking him.

AUTHOR. I didn't take offence.

MAN. You see: all that culture meant to me was Brahms in X sharp minor—

WIFE. There's no X sharp!

MAN. And a lot of stuck-up pansies showing off.

WIFE. George, George! It isn't true!

MAN. No? I'll swear some of them were. It never occurred to me that there might be something in it for me. . . . How do you do it? All those people?

AUTHOR. You enter into an arrangement with the audience. If they give you the green light, then you just think of these people and step into their skins. And if I believe it, then I find that the audience does, too.

MAN. You know that bit, in the second part, where that red light was winking—

AUTHOR. There was no red light.

MAN. I saw it!

AUTHOR. I'm glad, but there was no red light.

MAN. You sure? I'll swear I saw it.

AUTHOR. I think you've given me the answer to your question about culture. It's me talking, you listening, and your red light. It's not something rammed down your throat. It's something we do together, something shared. Does that answer you?

MAN. Yes, I think it does. Well: after-show time. What about a snort?

WIFE. Perhaps he's tired. . . .

AUTHOR, I'm not tired at all.

MAN. Draw up your chair. We'll see the night out.

AUTHOR. We talked until four in the morning. It was time for the next day's milk. I went with him; we had the whole herd done by eight. And he and his wife had talked more intimately that night than they may have done for years; I was only the agent. You get the picture: small town, big holding; too many cows. Two sons and a daughter; all left the district and glad to, as soon as their schooling was over; only come back twice a year now, with the grand-children at Christmas and Easter. Wife lonely and depressed, eating her heart out, just living from one CAS tour to the next, hungry for new faces and new ideas; her husband working harder than when he was starting out and not quite up to it, getting older and greyer and tireder. They're probably in better shape now, because of television but in the early sixties, when I was there, they had a grim life together.

INTERVIEWER. But to reach a man like that—

AUTHOR. He was good-hearted enough; no malice, really. And do you know, his coming to meet me, his seeing the red light, is the only criticism I have any time for? I don't mean I just wanted praise—not at all—but my piece either worked or it didn't, and that's the end of it. But when a man, any man, meets you in your work, along the axis of your imagination: well, it makes the whole thing seem worth it: the months away from home, the odd audience that doesn't kindle, making you feel a pretentious goat. That's the beauty of the form, you see; unless I reach George, it doesn't work at all.

INTERVIEWER. You talk of audiences that haven't kindled. Have you struck any that were actively hostile?

AUTHOR. Once or twice, in the early tours. I remember once in the South Island, trying to reach a group of young men who didn't know what they'd struck; they shifted and fidgeted and chattered, until—

INTERVIEWER. Until what?

AUTHOR. The race. Towards the end of *The Made Man*. And they came round afterwards, to apologise. One of them said that he'd seen himself, in this scene. But there was one real disturbance—

INTERVIEWER. When?

AUTHOR. Three years ago. I was performing in the Provincial Chambers, in Christchurch. It's a lovely hall and ideal for my piece, with a domed vaulted ceiling. When the lights dimmed on the beach at the end of Part I, I really seemed to be there, under the stars.

Well, this night, there was a party of Christ's College boys there, and the show seemed to be going well. About five minutes before the end, at the point where Firpo collapses there was a prolonged shout from the audience. I stopped, waited, then apologised to the audience and took it back a paragraph or two; got to the end without incident. After the show, I was visited by the master in charge of the Christ's College party who told me, a little primly, that none of his boys was responsible. Then my stage manager came in and said that a young man wanted to see me.

YOUNG MAN, *roughly dressed, sitting.*

YOUNG MAN. I'm cut. I'm three sheets in the wind.

AUTHOR, *approaching:* Did you call out? Was it you who made that noise?

YOUNG MAN *vaguely:* What noise?

AUTHOR. Someone shouted at me.

YOUNG MAN. I came all the way from Hokitika to see you. Room in a pub. Nine bob ticket. But I didn't come in till the end.

AUTHOR. Why?

YOUNG MAN *suddenly puts his head in his hands.*

AUTHOR. What's the matter? You all right?
YOUNG MAN *raising head:* You free?
AUTHOR. Yes.
YOUNG MAN. Come back to the pub for a bit? Got some beer in.
AUTHOR, *after a pause:* All right.

> *Six bottles of beer on dresser;* AUTHOR *sitting on bed,* YOUNG MAN *half lying across it.*

YOUNG MAN, *beer in hand:* Couldn't face it. When it came to the point there, couldn't face it.
AUTHOR. Why?
YOUNG MAN. Never had to face anything like that. In the flesh, like.
AUTHOR. I still don't get it.
YOUNG MAN. You know what I am? What I do?
AUTHOR. Not at a glance. Tell me.
YOUNG MAN. Deerstalker. Live in Hoky. Out three months at a time. Up on the tops, all on my own. Fit as a flea, no beer, no gut, no birds. Come down, cash my tails, live it up. All the grog, all the women I want. Gut out to here again. Then back up the tops, three months out, down again. Done it now, for five seasons.
AUTHOR. How old are you?
YOUNG MAN. Twenty-six. Why? Shocked?
AUTHOR. Shocked? No. What at?
YOUNG MAN. The killing. All that killing. Things that live, that have a right to live, I kill.
AUTHOR. I'm glad the Forest Service can't hear you.
YOUNG MAN. Killing: it's all I know. Killing. Setting your sights on a beautiful beast, bang and he's down. What comes then? Vietnam? Bigger and better kills?
AUTHOR. Then why did you come all this way, to see me?
YOUNG MAN. One night, I'm so cut, don't know Friday from breakfast. Cobber takes me to his place; give me a cup of coffee. Records on the shelf, mostly classical: can't stand the stuff, gets on my wick. Then I pick out this one

Record cover, The End of the Golden Weather Part I

you on the cover. Played it through. Then the other one.

Record Cover: The Made Man

Stayed there the whole week-end, playing them over and over. Then I bought them: played them over at home. Bought the book—

Book Cover, The End of the Golden Weather (1962)

Start a sentence. Go on: any sentence.

AUTHOR. Sentence?

YOUNG MAN. Anything from *Golden Weather*. Anything: you start it, I'll finish it.

AUTHOR. 'One Sunday morning, I am early on the beach and meet—'

YOUNG MAN. 'The sun showing a rim above the pale sea. The breeze off the water is damp and warm. I sniff its soft, salty breath: summer is in the air.' Right?

AUTHOR. Dead right. You know it all?

YOUNG MAN. Every bloody word. Learned it on the tops; said it over and over, round a fire, till I had it off.

AUTHOR. I'm staggered. It was hard enough for me to learn.

YOUNG MAN, *slightly challenging:* I've only had fifth-form education.

AUTHOR. So?

YOUNG MAN. And my opinion won't mean bugger-all to you.

AUTHOR. Try me.

YOUNG MAN. But you showed me that summer was not just a season, but a climate of the mind.

AUTHOR. If you can see that and say it like that, then you don't need more than fifth-form education.

YOUNG MAN. Come off it. I'm an ignorant hooer.

AUTHOR. It's probably the best thing that's ever been said about it. One I'll remember when I've forgotten all the others.

YOUNG MAN. Okay, I see it; I say it. Now what?

AUTHOR. What do you mean? What do you want to do?

YOUNG MAN. I don't want to go on just killing, that's for sure.

AUTHOR. Then, that's a start, isn't it?

YOUNG MAN. Yeh, it's a start. First step like.

He takes a long swig, then begins muttering softly: 'The broom is almost bare of flowers and, as I watch—

His hand rises.

a jaundiced bloom flutters off the bush and, sustained by the light breeze, charts a hazy course before coming to rest beside me.'

He leans down over the bed and gropes for an imaginary flower

'I pick it up and—

AUTHOR *in performance*

AUTHOR, . . . 'somehow I know, as I finger the jaded petals, that

summer

is quite

at an

end.'

★

The End

of the Golden

Weather

★

I INVITE YOU TO JOIN ME IN A VOYAGE INTO THE PAST, TO THAT territory of the heart we call childhood. Consider, if you will, Te Parenga. A beach, three-quarters of a mile long, a hundred yards wide at low water. Rocks at either end: on the east, chunky and rounded, a squat promontory. The "king" and "queen" stand a few yards out from the shore: two squashed rock pillars with steps cut into their sides for diving in the summer. At high water, the sea will cover more than half of them. The rocks on the west are shallow, spreading into a terraced reef, shelving far out to sea. Here there is no smoothness. The surface of these rock shelves is jagged, cutting and tearing at the bare foot, fretted away by the corrosive sea. The receding tide leaves deep pools here where sea anemones with fronts of red and black jelly wave coloured strings to entice the shrimps, and sometimes a lone starfish lies marooned, diminishing in the sun. Ahead, across a narrow channel, central to vision and imagination, Rangitoto, enormous, majestic, spread-eagled on the skyline like a sleeping whale, declining from a central cone to the water in two huge flanges, meeting the sea in a haze of blue and green. It guards Te Parenga from wind and tempest: it has a brooding splendour.

The beach is fringed with *pohutukawa* trees, single and stunted in the gardens, spreading and noble on the cliffs, and in the empty spaces by the foreshore. Tiny red coronets prick through the grey-green leaves. Bark, flower and leaf seem overlaid by smoke. The red is of a dying fire at dusk, the green faded and drab. Pain and age are in these gnarled forms, in bare roots,

31

clutching at the earth, knotting on the cliff-face, in tortured branches, dark against the washed sky.

Beside this majesty, the houses of Te Parenga have a skimped look. A low ridge curls upwards from the beach, flattening to accept the concrete ribbon of the main road north, an intermittent rash of shops on its margins, then the ridge rolls on and down to the mud-flats and mangroves of the upper harbour. The houses of Te Parenga face the sea, unlovely bungalows of wood and tin, painted red and brown to thwart the rodent air. At the end of the beach, before the main road north leaves it for ever a clot of buildings: shops, banks, the Council Chambers, the Anglican Church in wooden Gothic, cheek by jowl with the cinema—built to last—in brick.

It's only a hundred years since men dressed as chimneys, in top hats and black stove-pipes, women dressed as great bells, tiny feet as clappers, stepped ashore at Te Parenga from a broad-bellied, wind-billowed ship. They brought with them grain and root, tilling and harvest; timber trees, fruit trees, flowers, shrubs, grass; sheep, cows, horses, deer, pigs, rabbits, fish, bees; language, law, custom, clocks and coinage; Queen Victoria and her views on Heaven and Earth; The Trinity; Santa Claus and the imagery of snow where no snow will ever fall at Christmas; a thousand years of history, a shoal of shibboleths, taboos and prohibitions and the memory of a six-months' voyage. They threw them all together in a heap and stepped ashore to slash the bush, banish the natives and pray silently far into the night. They left some of the pohutukawas, and Rangitoto was beyond their reach.

This is Te Parenga: my heritage, my world.

Sunday

at

Te Parenga

SUNDAY IS THE BEST DAY AT TE PARENGA. I AM ALWAYS UP early on Sundays, run down the path that snakes round the *karaka* tree and the flax bushes, jump down the steps on to the beach. The sand is a cold grey powder, slow-seeping between the toes. At this hour before the sun is up, the beach is bathed in a cold glow, lucid, but dead. This early Sunday half-world is the territory of the "characters", who come from hiding to spread their strangeness like plumage on the hospitable, silver air. There, kicking a stone before him, is the Reverend Thirle, mumbling his sermon. Mumbling, he kicks the flat pebble before him, stalking it intently, as if it were a tiring mouse. His aim is often wild and the stone shoots into the sea, lapped around by a lacy spume; he dances on the edge like a heron, clerical-black arms flapping, so I rush down and pick it out, wipe it on my pants, and hand it back to him.

"Ah. Thank you, my boy," he says in his northern voice. "Lose that, and I'm sunk."

"Are you? Why?"

He looks at it reflectively, affectionately.

"It's a talisman. Had it for years. Helps me to think! Kick this along. I'm all right. My thoughts flow."

He gives me a bland, quizzical look.

"I call it Peter. Do you know why?"

Peter? I shake my head.

He swells and strikes a pose, his fist upraised.

"Because the Church is built on a rock called Peter!"

"Oh," I say doubtfully, "is it?"

"Here. That's a joke. You're meant to laugh."

I titter, dutifully, feebly.

"Well, thank you for the applause! Here, I must be off. Know your catechism?"

A swirl of archaic English floods into my head.

"Nearly," I tell him, bravely.

"Good lad. See you later, won't I?"

He won't, but I don't tell him this. He throws the stone called Peter before him and hops off after it, roaring at the assembled elements of earth, air, and water: "I tell ye, ye're like lost sheep!" The voice fades, and he is gone.

Over there, by our steps, Miss Effie Brett has waddled on to the beach. She is supposed to weigh more than twenty stone. Barefooted, huge and rock-faced, dressed in a long calico shift untethered at the waist, she looks as if she is about to be baptised in some outlandish cult. Her hair hangs long and straight over her shoulders, and her eyes have a stony calm. She walks to the water's edge, letting the sea-froth play over her feet, raises her arms above her head and locks her hands. One leg, as solid and shapeless as a jetty pile, slowly rises, as if she were a gigantic ballerina, limbering up. Then she sees me and runs towards me on her toes, suddenly curiously dainty and finicky, stops and stares at me.

"Nice day," she shouts in my face.

"Yes, Miss Effie," I say nervously, not daring to look at her.

"How's your mother?" she roars, peering at me through the loose hanks of hair.

"She's very well, thank you, Miss Effie."

I know what's coming.

"Drunk again?" she screams, with a leer of satisfaction. Yes, that was it: always the same.

"I don't know what you mean, Miss Effie."

"Ask Sybil: she knows! Ask Sybil!"

Miss Effie and her sister Miss Sybil Brett, live in Massey Street just behind us. One day, when my mother was going to the shops, Miss Effie leaned out of the window and screamed: "She drinks, that woman: she drinks!" Then Miss Sybil appeared briefly, wrenched Miss Effie away, the sound of a sharp slap and fierce yelling. My mother was shocked and upset, but it never happened again; Miss Sybil, a fiercely withdrawn, gaunt little woman, watched over her sister like a gaoler. But once a week, early on Sunday mornings, she was set at liberty and roamed huge and untamed on the beach until a long blast on a whistle called her home. It came now, shrill and piercing.

The great body shivers; the head rears up like some alarmed and cornered animal.

"Goodbye, goodbye!" she shouts and gallops off like a fastidious buffalo, whacking her flank as if she were her own jockey. I shiver. Miss Effie belongs to a different and terrifying race.

Along by the rocks on the east end, a figure crouches in the smooth wet sand digging for *pipis*.[1] This is Firpo, the butt of the beach, thin as a spoon, with unshaven flaccid cheeks and bulging fear-strewn eyes, dressed in dirty jeans and the top half of a tattered woollen bathing suit, button gone on the shoulder so that one strap hangs loose, exposing the bony rib-cage. I go up to him. He sees my legs, looks up, his face all feverish animation.

"Gidday, boy! Early birds, aren't we? How's tricks?"

"All right, Firpo."

"Want to help get Firpo's breakfast?"

He always talks like this, as if he were someone else.

I kneel down beside him. The pipis hide in the shining wet strip where the sea runs up and back; little bubbles escape from their lairs, flawing and pocking the sand. We scoop out the handfuls of sodden grit and there, dully gleaming, are the pipis, tiny yellow tongues slowly retracting, as if their alarm at approaching dissolution were slight. Firpo's flax basket is almost full.

"How's the training, Firpo?" I ask him, at length.

Firpo starts, his eyes blink, jumps up and beats his chest.

"Fit! Fit! Fit as a fighting tomcat, Firpo is!"

He begins a strenuous full-knees bend, arms outstretched,

---

[1] *pipis.* Shellfish found in the sand on New Zealand beaches.

palms up, tottering and precarious, shouting at me to admire his skill. Suddenly, he pauses, arrested in mid-bend, stands up, rigid, and I follow his gaze. Bouncing towards us over the sand is Jesse Cabot, heavyweight wrestling champion of the British Empire, a Canadian who has come for the season to Te Parenga. He stumps along, a huge chubby baby in white shorts; a gaudy bath-robe flares out behind him, sustained in the light, morning breeze. In each great hand he holds a rock, bearing them before him like offerings to the gods, their weight bulging and distending his huge biceps; ropes of knotted veins course down his neck like swollen underground streams. He looks straight ahead, olympian and majestic, his heels deeply indenting the sand in a widely spaced, double track. Firpo looks suddenly strained and old, and his bulging eyes water.

"Gotta get along, eh," he mutters enigmatically and walks off, hunched and tormented.

The sun comes up over the cliff, a bland unwinking disc— heralding a bright, explicit world. The characters have melted away, as though the full light were not their element. The beach is deserted. My brother calls me from the steps. Breakfast.

By ten o'clock, the people of Te Parenga are abroad, liberated for a day from their caged bondage in buildings or at sinks. The beach is spattered with their clots of colour and spurting with their talk. The sea rolls on and up the sand, frothing near the grey powder by the gates and Te Parenga settles into its Sunday ravishment by sun and sea.

Promptly at eleven, Sergeant Robinson appears on the beach. He has been Te Parenga's sergeant of police for over thirty years. Small, fierce-eyed, round and gnarled as a nut, he strides along with a nuggety grandeur, clean white Sunday shirt blazing, no tie, helmet set just a trifle askew to show that he is not on duty, striped braces straining like hawsers over his shoulders, bowing, saluting, regally acknowledging salvoes of greetings from all over the beach.

A new fashion has recently reached Te Parenga. For the first time, men have begun to appear on the beach in shorts and are no longer encased from neck to upper thigh. This offends Robbie's deeply Victorian sense of propriety. Again and again I recall scenes like this:

"Aw, gidday, Bill. Aw, not so bad. Heat gets yer. Gets all mucky, under me helmet. . . . What's that? Gubberment? Well, whaddya expect with them jokers down a Wellington. . . . Hey! Hey, you! And where do you think you're going. What? For a walk? Like that? All uncovered on ya top? Ya not decent! Cover yaself up, quick and lively. All a yas! Cover yaselves up!"

He lumbers off, muttering: "Think this is a nudiest colony, a somethin. . . ."

And the men comply with towels until he has moved on, when bare flesh again emerges to barks of laughter, but not so that Robbie can hear, for he is greatly admired and respected on the beach.

"Ya gotta hand it to him, though," is the universal tribute, "proper ole dag. . . ."

The golden day seeps on; no thoughts but warm, no talk but trivial, until the sun fingers the eyeballs dead ahead—the sand cools, and the beach slowly empties.

On Sunday nights in the summer, we have tea on the glassed-in verandah facing Rangitoto. My mother prepares a mountain of sandwiches and out they come, mounds of them, on a jingling trolley. There we sit in the summer, while the day ends in gold explosions on the horizon and the lower borders of the sky are suddenly drenched in pink, as though a full brush had been slapped round the rim. Below us on the beach, people are strolling and the thin rarefied tinkle of their voices floats up to us as they approach, then a sudden blare of coherent sound. . . .

"So I said to Phyllis, what's the use? Why don't you finish with him, for good and all. . . ."

Will Phyllis give him up?

Or this, in a high, fluty voice:

"Well, I went to her house and everything on the line was silk and I thought, Mmmm-mm! Mine's cotton. . . ."

Or an urgent foreign voice:

"But Hans, why did you do it? What were you thinking of. . . ?"

What had the man done, so far from home? . . . Huge questions, teasing the mind for ever. Laughter like a rocket burst, hanging on the still air in showers of sparks. . . .

Tonight, we have guests and, as always, we scream for charades as soon as it is dark. The signal given, the evening falls together like old ritual. My brother and I perform a few curtain-raisers like "hen-peck" and "hand-cuff", acting out the first syllable, the second and then the whole word. Then we politely ask the guests to perform, some shrinking and terrified, looking for the nearest sofa to hide under; others consent and perform with a touching bravado and sit down, looking sheepish, so we applaud with vigour, saying "Jolly good!" in a kindly way, so they won't feel too shown up, later. For we are only waiting for the supreme moment when we can ask our father to play. He looks at us over his glasses, thoughtful and mischievous; we rush at him in an agony, each seizing a knee and pulling it outwards with our entreaty, as if to split him. After a moment of torturing indecision he consents and retires; from the kitchen comes the rattle of utensils. We giggle, nudge each other and throw knowing looks at the guests.

In bursts my father, swivelling round corners, Chaplin-wise, bowler-hatted, frock-coated, holding a bulging and jingling carpet-bag. He advances on his victim, the light of self-abandoned frenzy in his eye, speaking in a voice of comic heaviness and briskness:

"Come here, come here, come here! Don't like your colour! Looks like a bad case of hydrangea! Put out your tongue!"

He seizes the organ delicately, shakes his head. His eyes gleam with a terrible zeal.

"Oh ho ho ho! This is serious! Convolvulus has set in. We must operate at once!"

The victim is hustled off his chair, screaming with laughter and thrown flat on a table; tries to rise, but the mad doctor presses his head. The patient crumples. A fearsome jingling from the carpet-bag.

"Now, now, what's best for the incision? Ah ha! The very thing. My tenon-saw. Don't worry, don't worry! It'll only tickle!"

The victim struggles to sit up: the doctor flattens him with an imperious gesture. He saws furiously, making a ghastly, ticking scratching sound.

"Now that didn't hurt, did it? Stop laughing! Pin back the flaps . . . that's the way. . . . Now we have to dig. Get at the root of the trouble. Where's my garden trowel?"

He drops the saw, seizes the trowel, makes great swooping motions with it.

"Intestines? No use to you. Better without them." He throws them over his head. In horror, we see long loops and festoons of them sailing round the room, lodging on the clock, hanging on the pictures, whirling round and round the light bracket.

He digs again, ferociously.

"Heart? Lungs? Kidneys? Liver? Useless lumber. Out they go."

He throws them at the wall: we hear a hideous squelch. He looks down at his patient, benevolently.

"Why, you're looking better already. Now, we'll sew you up. Here's my skewer. Thread it with a piece of string, and away we go!"

He becomes a maddened seamstress, frenziedly sewing, the skewer flying in and out. He dusts his hands, dismisses his patient.

"Go thou, and sin no more."

He bows to us, cold and dignified.

"Adieu. Adieu! Remember me!"

He grabs his carpet-bag, whirls on one leg, stops suddenly.

"What's this on my lapel? A stray kidney? Tt-tt-tt."

He flicks it off with a lordly air and whirls off on some other fearsome errand.

41

Gasping, we scream for more, but there is always only one. In a moment, he returns as himself, looking at us over his glasses with the mildest of airs and we gaze at him with astonishment and awe, that beneath that genial mask there lurks, crouching to spring, that ferocious doctor.

The guests depart and we prepare for bed, the wind faintly rustling the trees outside, platoons of moths hurling themselves at the lighted panes and the moon coyly showing a gleaming finger-nail paring above the dark mass of Rangitoto.

The night

of the

riots

THE DAYS OF CHILDHOOD SLOWLY THREAD THROUGH MEMORY like a golden snake, deeply scoring the mind, each day joined to the next by unbreakable filament. So one thinks, until the thread does break and the snake falls to bits, each piece meaningless and without connection. The night of the riots.

The first I knew of it was being woken by my father pounding down the hall, waving the morning paper.

"Look!" he shouted. "They've wrecked the city!"

I rushed into the bedroom. "What's happened?"

"Read it for yourself: you're old enough," said my father, pushing the paper at me. There I read that every window in Queen Street had been smashed during the night by a lawless mob, surging through the streets, looting and defying the police.

"Why did they do it?"

"Oh it's a long story," said my father, but my mother began to talk of hunger, of depression and relief and how it was a crying shame. . . .

"You should have been a trade unionist," said my father tersely and went off to shave.

Depression. Relief. I knew these words: had heard them at school. There were boys there without shoes who had bread and dripping for lunch and sometimes I would give them one of my sandwiches, sodden with fried egg or tomato, and feel a virtuous glow. But I never related it to my own world, bounded as it was by an unchanging security and when Mr Thirle read from the pulpit of the land of milk and honey, I thought it was my own. Milk we had, honey we had. And then men came to the back door, every day, selling junk out of battered suitcases and my mother had to say again and again that she wanted nothing. And the pinched, drawn faces, creased into sickly and plausible lines by constant rebuff—I saw them, yet still I was not shaken. There was Us, safe and solid, warm at night and there was Them—hungry and persistent, but separated from us by an uncrossable gulf. And now a whole city had exploded into wildness and savagery. . . . I went off to school that day heavy with a new load.

Everyone there was talking about it. Ginger Finucane hissed in my ear: "Hey, you know what? My Dad, he's in the riot last night; come home with two bottles of whisky—blotto at six in the morning!" At interval, Roy Baker came up to me and lowered his voice.

"Hey, there's gunna be a demonstration down Te Parenga tonight, down by the Council Buildings, and I'm going down there too, see if I can pick anything up!"

My whole body flooded suddenly with fear and excitement.

"What about the police?"

"Police? Ya mean ole Robbie? Aw, he couldn't stop anything. Wouldn't want to, either. He's a good ole stick. Anyway, he'll be over in town. They called them all up. That's why we're trying it on here. . . ."

I held this knowledge to me like a secret and dreadful crime. I came home with it oozing from me like a stain, feeling that my mother must see it, gasp with horror and reach for a towel to wipe it off, but she gave me a biscuit as usual and sent me to the beach. At six, my father came home bearing a mysterious slim parcel—as I looked through the French doors into his room, I saw him unwrap it and hang it on the bedpost—a wooden club, and this symbol of violence suddenly explicit in our house gave me a tingling shock.

My parents read the paper and discussed the news in the low grey voices adults reserve for death or horror when children are within earshot. My father spoke of a jeweller's shop smashed open the night before and a man shouting "Help yaselves, girls!"

and two women scooping up handfuls of rings, bracelets and necklaces. My already fevered imagination pictured them: I could see them as if I had been there—dyed red hair, shapeless chalk-white faces, welts like clowns where their lips should be, fat and noisy, dropping jewels like glittering stars down the clefts of their bulging bosoms.

We were sent to bed early, but I lay awake. My brother and I shared the verandah in the summer—what were two couches by day became our beds at night. I looked over at him, slowly subsiding into sleep and wondered if I should tell him of the awful plan in my mind, but he was only ten—would not have understood. Then he began the faint wheezing which told me he was beyond my reach. I lay awake, my hands over my eyes to keep them firmly fixed on my plan while the house slowly hushed; my parents went to bed, muttered for a while, then total silence.

I let this silence tingle about me, heavy with portent, for about half an hour, prayed briefly and desperately, shifted my weight carefully to avoid creaks, took my clothes to the kitchen and put them on, turned the key softly in the back door and slipped out. Down the path to the beach I ran, along the soft sand that led to the Strand, the Council Buildings and the shops, sticking to the No Man's Land in the middle of the road that the light couldn't reach, shot across the street like a fleeing rabbit, eased my way along the wall of the Council Buildings and peered round.

At the junction of two roads, there was an overhead light and it shone down on about twenty men gathered there, the light on their heads turning their eyes into holes, sharply outlining the cheekbones, deeply scoring the loose folds of crêpy necks. No sign of Roy Baker and—he had been wrong about the police for there was Robbie, mounted, baton in hand, thickset and stern, his face square and remote. The horse picked its way up and down among the men with a delicate precision; they glowered at it and muttered as he passed. And each man held in his hand a stone which he looked at tenderly, then back at the policeman. I thought of David and Goliath except that here were twenty

Davids, all middle-aged, but the tingling menace of this scene came not from them, but from the thick, silent figure on the horse.

One of the men raised his arm suddenly. The policeman tugged at the reins and the horse wheeled.

"Now I've told yas before an' I'll say it again. The first a yous jokers starts anything lands in gaol. So make up ya minds whosit gunna be. I got powers here, an' I can use them. . . ."

"Aw lissun, Robbie. . . ."

"Sergeant!"

"Aw, break it down, Robbie. . . ."

"Ya get nothin' outa me, 'less ya call me right name."

A mutinous shuffle: muttering.

"Wull, Sergeant, then. . . . How long since you had a good square meal?"

Robbie swelled suddenly.

"None a ya damn' business!"

"Aw, tonight, a course," came a thin, pinched voice. "Look at that puk!¹ Big fat slob."

"An' I want none a ya lip, neither!" Robbie thundered. "I may be a nole joker, but I got me job here. Keep law n'order, 'n youse fullas outa mischief. An' by Christ I will, if I got to put the whole lottyas in clink!"

He swivelled the horse and his eyes balefully, then seemed to sort out faces, people he knew. He softened to a weary reasonableness.

"Now, look. Why don't yas all go home? Is it gunna help the Missus or ya kids if ya land in clink and face a charge? I got nothin' 'gainst you jokers. Just I got my orders: have to do my job."

"Ye know what my kids et tonight?" came a Scottish voice. "One boiled spud each. One boiled spud!"

"Yeh, mine too! There's ya land of milk and honey for ya!"

"God's Own Country!" and the scornful voice was Irish. "Jesus!"

---

1 Puk: contraction of *puku,* a Maori word meaning belly; much used by both races.

Robbie seemed to explode, suddenly.

"Well, I'm not responsible! Ya can't blame me! Ya gotta leave it to those jokers down at Wullington! There's no other way".

There was a silence and then an oldish man who seemed to be some kind of a leader said: "Ah, the ole bastard's right. Only doin' his job. Doin' na good here. C'mon. Let's get along.'

There was a shuffling, then a sudden concerted move. The stones clattered to the road and the grey-faced, eyeless men passed out of the light, silent, beaten, their spirit as motley and incoherent as their shuffling walk. The policeman sat on his horse motionless, the light falling on his helmet. His face showed neither pain nor pleasure, neither scorn nor pity. Then he put his heels into his horse's flanks—I shrank as he shot past my hiding-place and the gallops declined to a faint, clinking patter in the dark.

Silence. I came out from behind the wall, stood for a moment in the light. There was a little cairn of stones in the middle of the street. I kicked at it, suddenly: stones scuttled away from me, rattled into the gutter.

I crept home along the beach, let myself into the house, changed and slipped back into bed. For a long time I lay awake. An iron grille had clanged shut on my mind. I could still see through its bars the receding landscape of childhood, immured there, pure and shining. Ahead, the multi-coloured adult world, Man's Own Country, studded with grim effigies marked Greed, Authority, Pride and Law—armour to be assumed for adult occasions. And humour: kindness: sacred and redeeming graces as I had seen them and loved them in the old policeman—how easily, how willingly extinguished!

That night marked an end: the end of the golden weather.

Christmas

at

Te Parenga

CHRISTMAS EVE: A DAY AS LONG AS A YEAR OF PENANCE. IN THE kitchen, my mother's face is flushed from the stove from which, all day, she has drawn forth cakes, scones, biscuits, mince pies; they stand on the bench outside, cooling in the shade, platoons of them, four abreast, marching into the barracks of abundance. My brother and I hide behind the door until our mother leaves the room; creep in like conspirators making the secret sign of their order, fingers crooked: scoop them into the bowls of icing, chocolate, lemon, vanilla and feel the cool, sharp flavours sting our tongues. Caught once, smacked, sent outside; caught twice, smacked harder, sent to the beach.

My father comes home early, springing without the weight of the year. A fortnight to go before he shoulders the next load of days. He changes into shorts, fills a glass with beer, bubbles with talk. As my mother passes him, weary, abstracted, he sweeps her on his knee, nuzzles in her neck. She screams and smacks him: the kitchen is full of laughter.

The long, long day falls at last along the beach; the darkening house is wrapped around with mystery. The moon peers above Rangitoto, drenching the lawn in a luminous spray, gilding the flax bushes and the *karaka* tree stands dark against a drained sky, every leaf soaked in portent. Everything promises, everything endows, with no question asked, no down-payment: only giving, only abundance. The world prepares to surrender its secret essence.

On the mantelpiece, a hundred cards shout greetings in a hundred scripts. Santa Claus, radish-cheeked, ice-blue eyed, his face a mask of merriment, guides his sleigh through flaking snow or pauses by a chimney, weighed down by magic freight. "Greetings, greetings, greetings. How's the wife, how' the kids, what's the news of Uncle Jim?" The world's voice rich, thick and loud raised in a mighty chorus of solicitude.

And I, pious and smug, my mind swilled clean with the foaming suds of goodwill, take my brother off to Church for Christmas Eve. The long nave sucks us down towards the altar, dim and ruddy-glowing; all round, devout dark heads bob on a trough of gloom, like corks on a mysterious sea.

Mr Thirle at the pulpit, a huge benign penguin. . . .
"Behold, a Virgin shall conceive, and bear a Son. . . ."
The Star, the Wise Men, While Shepherds Watched, Away in a Manger, The Child: the immemorial images softly fall, slowly sinking through the mind like distant jewels. A great bronze eagle on the pulpit, wings spread for flight, glares at the Book, daring it to be true. . . .

Prayer. Scrabbling for the hassock, joining the gritty chorus of penitence, like a vacuum-cleaner sucking up Sin. . . .
We-have-erred-and-strayed-from-Thy-ways-like-lost-sheep. . . .
Followed-too-much-the-devices-and-the-desires-of-our-own-hearts
. . . . Offended-against-Thy-Holy-Laws. . . .
"How?" asks my brother, puzzled. I give him a look. Impious little. . . . "Sssh!"
And-there-is-no-health-in-us. . . .
No health. No health! Just two sick boys, stuffed with sin, packed tight with evil, and joy! flooding them; sweeping them out of the church on an abundant tide; jumping, dancing, watching; the grotesque obediences of their shadows, enlarging, contracting; doubling suddenly when two lights converge to form a pool, each struggling to retain the image, fading and dissipating as the two Unhealthy Sinners rush on.

Home to the hushed house, dense with being: pillowslips, limp and slack, palely glaring at the ends of the beds. . . .

*Behold - a - pillowslip - shall - conceive - and - bear - presents - before-
morning; The-Straight-shall-be-crooked-and-the-Plain-Places-
Rough. . . .*

A large star hangs lamp-like in the East to guide the merry
saint; the long slide into sleep down a chute sprinkled with fray-
ing snow. Rest on the snowdrift, thick and deep with a red sleigh
crossing it like a moving gobbet of blood and in the far, far
distance, a tiny chime of bells. . . .

Christmas morning. The dead pillowslips alive, miraculously
quickened in the night: the Word made bulging Flesh. Tearing
of paper, shouting: turning keys in clockwork innards, stifling
chagrins that the watch isn't real, that the doll doesn't speak—
warning noises from the bedroom: "Don't disturb; your mother's
tired"—creeping in to see if it's true; weary, bleary parents, faces
tight with tiredness and the effort of goodwill at five in the morning. Laughter crackling and spouting. Love . . . love.

By ten o'clock on Christmas morning, the sun wraps Te
Parenga round like a hot oilskin, searing the back under shirts,
stinging bare arms and legs. A clear green sea edges up the beach
in finicky slaps like a coy woman, marking its progress in half-
hoops of delicate froth. We rush to immerse ourselves in the
glittering element, shouting "Merry Christmas!" to our parents'
friends, watching their faces narrowly for signs of Grace. Will
Mr Johnson's hard old dial, as blank as a prison wall, fissure and
crack with the earthquake of a smile? No, it won't. But at least
he mutters through closed, thin lips: "Merry Christmas, lad."
Oh, and look at crabby old Miss Mackay! who never ventures
further in than ankle depth, never allows herself more pleasure
than a cold dour sluice of her mottled, flesh-rippling shoulders,
or a hand-scoop of sea to slosh into her cavernous armpits—
look at her now, moving slowly and majestically out to sea,
powered by an antique breaststroke, a noble and dignified old
whale. And out we come, dripping and gleaming, our souls
unsullied white in this glorious no-past, no-future: only the im-
maculate present, endlessly pouring its essence on us.

The parade begins. Sergeant Robinson arrives, buttoned to the
neck in official serge, his helmet set dead-centre, his two Boer

War medals flashing, clinking over his heart, bowing, saluting, puffing and stamping through the sand. Jesse Cabot appears, in the full rig of a British Empire Champ, towelled robe of red, white and blue coiling stripes, his silver belt, emblem of prowess, locked round his waist, rocks in hands, red moon-face split by a huge pithy grin, like an orange with a smile cut on it. He prances along, physical man incarnate, a huge success—behind him, the admiring chorus: "By God, Jesse's getting fit. Even on Christmas Day! Gunna keep that belt again!" Miss Effie and Miss Sybil emerge for morning service, clad in long robes of rusty black velvet and white canvas shoes, Miss Effie in a huge black picture hat salvaged from some Victorian relation, looking as if she is on her way to a spectral garden fête in honour of the dead. Miss Sybil's hat is a squashed black dome from which a few grey tendrils stray in a mop-like fringe. Miss Effie bounds along, shouting, laughing, crouches in the sand, turns and waits; Miss Sybil, urgent and gawky, marches up behind her, prods her in the back with a ferruled stick; up she jumps, skips and dances on.

The day moves on, so white and generous that nothing must sully it. "What! Tears on Christmas Day! What! Quarrelling on Christmas Day!" as though on any other day these sins were venial but today, mortal. Every irritant, however slight, is mercilessly held up to show its hideous blackness on the white sheet of Christmas. Peace on Earth! for twenty-four hours. Fatigue shall be banished, discomfort shall not be admitted. Smiles will be fixed on Christmas Day and worn like honourable decorations until the clock striking twelve, proclaims release.

The feast. Table gleaming white, laid with silver implements in squads! At each place a coloured cracker, dribbling fringes at both ends, ready for its volley of tiny ordnance. The turkey, sacrificial bird, shorn limbs folded, demure in death, borne aloft to the sound of toy trumpets, majestic breast like a proud mountain ridge, golden-crumb encrusted. The pudding, dark and tacky, rich and thick, blue smoke racing round its brow at a touch of flame. Surfeit and abundance. Bellies like sinkers.

At one-thirty p.m., the temperature reads 88 degrees in the shade. . . .

After dinner, the mountain of dishes lies ignored; my parents, winded and grounded by the subsiding ballast of goodwill, escape into sleep. My brother disappears towards the beach, ignoring my entreaties to stay and help. For tonight—is the concert. A cloud of apprehension descends and wreathes about me, flapping limply and damply across my belly, sitting on my head like a soft aqueous sponge.

For weeks we have been preparing it. My sister, nine, is pliable and loyal, but my brother is furiously contemptuous, refusing to perform at all. I bribe him with chocolate fish and changing balls and when he is quite sure that all my pocket money is gone, he agrees—graciously—to perform in the play, specially written! on condition that his part shall not exceed two words. Groaning under this enormous obstacle, I comply. He is to make a single entrance, say "Hullo, Dad!" and depart, never to be seen again.

Programme:

Piano solo: *Soldiers' March,* by Schumann—my sister.
Piano solo: *Minuet in G,* by Paderewski—me.
Piano duet: *Intro and Galop*—both of us.

INTERVAL,

while my sister rushes to the kitchen to wriggle into last year's pink *tutu* and grab a frilly basket full of rose petals, which she is to toss about to Mendelssohn's *Spring Song:* I have played it for her over a hundred times while my mother and she sweated out the steps. Then the play, called *By Love Deliver'd* and Grand Finale, ten historical tableaux under the title of *Living Waxworks* for which spaces are left in the programme for the audience to guess. Prize: a threepenny bar of chocolate.

God Save the King.

Nervous inside, as though a whole cage of sparrows twittered and fluttered there, I spend the afternoon with my sister, setting out costumes and properties, rigging up the sliding curtains on the French doors which give on to the verandah where the audience will sit.

As the day expires in eruptions of splendour in the west, my parents emerge from sleep and like wan shades of the dead, pass dazedly through the motions of washing up. The turkey lies there ruined and gaping, its proud façade eroded, a strut of bones, hung with tatters of flesh. We tear these off and press them between pieces of bread and butter; my mother tersely explains: "You'll get no more today."

At seven, we set up the chairs on the verandah in rows and the guests arrive, Indian files of them, snaking up the path from the beach and I am suddenly appalled at the power each one contains within to wreck the evening by misplaced laughter. Soon they are assembled and seated; the men with jugs of beer to their hands, the women with smaller tumblers of coloured liquids laced with gin, the kids with cordial. My heart thumping, I stand close to the curtain and hear for the first time that anticipatory buzz, at once so promising and so—menacing. They are no longer an assembly of friends I have known since I was born but a hydra-headed monster of unknown temper to be wooed, cajoled, placatèd, appeased. My brother, uneasily sharing my tenseness in the suspended animation of our quarters back-stage, suddenly thrusts his head between the curtains and makes a face. Screams and cheering. I lunge at him in fury, venom in my heart.

I pull on the curtain with trembling hand; it parts in little womanish jerks then closes again—in my flurry, I have pulled the wrong cord. It parts. Cheers. My sister enters, demure and pink-cheeked, a bow in her hair and plays her Schumann with a softly radiant poise I marvel at. I follow, my mouth dry, my eyes wild and unfocussed, rattling through the Paderewski as if I were an unwilling tourist in a foreign country, concerned only to make the hated journey up and down the pages as fast as possible. I get bogged on the last page, skip twenty bars, stop; with a sudden flash of inspiration do four furious *glissandi* up and down the keyboard with my thumbnail and land with a crash on the tonic chord. I smile bleakly at the faces, as drained of personality as round cheeses, hanging there in the dark like hostile planets and then my sister and I play our duet at a speed that leaves us gasping. While my sister changes, I stand close to the curtain to hear what they are saying about the concert, and about me. . . .

"No it's funny; haven't heard from Joyce this year. . . ."

"Aw, wull, if they put up the prices any more I just won't buy, and that'll teach 'em! . . ."

"Come on, come on! Drink up! Have the hair of the dog that bit ya. . .!"

Curtain up again.

I stalk grimly to the piano and strike up. My sister flashes in from the kitchen, a frilly, pink, smiling sausage, her straight fair hair leaping out from her head. She hops and turns, jumps and lands, throwing rose petals out into the audience where they descend in a soft velvet shower, lodging in hair and ears, tickling necks or making graceful landings on beer-froth and gin-and-orange. Cheers, whistles and stamps. They want it again! "No more petals," says my sister, showing her empty basket. So the petals are collected! one by one, salvaged from beery and ginny graves and away we go on the *Spring Song* again.

The play. I am a sick old man, rejuvenated by the love of a pure young girl. I wear a beard and bowler hat until the moment of apotheosis when, transformed by love, I shed both to reveal the downy cheeks of a twelve-year-old boy. One line only I recall because of how it was received. The old man gives a wheezing cough then says dourly: "Dunno wot's the matter with me; must need a pill." A great wave of laughter leaps out of the audience, a sudden immersing flood. "Try fruit salts!" they call. "Be regular! Be a Merry Andrew!" but these pleasantries I hardly hear for this is the moment of my brother's entrance. No sign of him. I hiss his name. Still nothing. I flash a sickly smile towards

THE END OF THE GOLDEN WEATHER

the audience and rush to the kitchen door. He is there, reading a comic. "You are on!" I tell him in a screaming whisper. I jump back to my place, resume my pose as old man, bent and tottering, palsied hand on stick. My brother saunters in from the kitchen, winks at the audience, looks at me in a sudden panic. He has forgotten his two words! I mouth them at him, my jaw aching with my furious pantomime. Nothing. Then suddenly impish and grotesque, he performs a little jig, pokes his tongue out at the audience and capers off. The laughter is loud and long. "Proper little comedian that," I hear someone say. I glare at the dark, dread and hatred warring in me, somehow bring the play to an end. As soon as the curtain is across, I rage and fume. "Aw, give it a bone," he counters amiably.

Living waxworks. My sister climbs into a wire waste-paper basket, draped in a Japanese kimono: she is to be Queen Elizabeth and I Sir Walter Raleigh, laying down the cloak. My brother, who is to be our page, in white bathing top and satin bloomers, suddenly seizes the Queen's rope wig which took days to tease out, plumps it on his head awry and appears before the curtain, smirking and grimacing. The audience, somewhat dazed, begin scribbling on their papers. "No, no!" I scream, only half into my Walter Raleigh breeches, "it hasn't started yet!" I turn on my brother, goaded now beyond endurance and punch him in the stomach. He gasps with pain and punches me back. We are on the floor, a mass of whirling limbs and I hear my breeches rip. My father rushes in and separates us. We stand in tears, gasping, speechless. "And now shake hands, boys, because it's still Christmas Day, you know," he commands. We touch hands, gulping with dry sobs. My ears are flaps of fire, my heart jumps.

My sister and I struggle in and out of ten different costumes: Queen Elizabeth, Magna Carta, Arthur Losing his Eyes, When Did You Last See Your Father?, The Relief of Lucknow ("dinna ye hear it?"), Charles I Losing his Head. The lights go on in the verandah and the guests smoke and chatter. My brother, now sulky and subdued, collects the answers.

Uncle Jim prances in, very gay and noisy.

"Jolly good!" he shouts.

I stare at him stonily and turn away. He biffs me on the back so that my head jerks, my eyes smart. "Oh, come on! Cheer up, boy! We're a long time dead, you know!"

I ignore him and settle down dourly to mark the answers and Uncle Jim, after a moment of fidgeting and indecision, creeps out. Laugher on the verandah. I look at the answers. "Mutt and Jeff", I read. "Jiggs and Maggie. Laurel and Hardy." I put my head in my hands. My sister proceeds, calmly marking. "Auntie Kass has two right," she announces at least. "Then give her the prize," I say heavily, no longer caring. The prize. Where is the prize? I rush on to the verandah. Uncle Jim is eating it! My sister, quite unruffled, announces: "Auntie Kass has won the prize but naughty Uncle Jim is eating it! For that he'll have to buy her a sixpenny bar of chocolate!" But this I hardly hear because I am in tears again. . . .

The fog of anguish lifts, our friends disperse. My brother and I are sent to the beach, to cool off and make it up. I am silent, still grappling with wedges of fury. "Why did you do it? Why did you have to go and spoil it all?" I rasp out at him. He pauses a moment, trying to find words.

"Listen . . . I was . . . scared."

I look at him in wonder.

"Scared. Scared! . . . Were you?"

He looks up at me shamefaced, nods.

I am suddenly calm. Some hint of the complexity of human motive and behaviour reaches me. He puts his hand into mine and we walk on in the dark, the sand firm and cold to our bare feet, the sea thumping down and expiring in long sussurations on the shingle, under the wide and healing arch of stars.

The

Made

Man

The time sequence of *The Made Man*
is somewhat longer than in Part I; the
opening of *The Made Man* begins at
a point of time previous to *Sunday
at Te Parenga* and ends at a point
later than *Christmas at Te Parenga.*
Thus the narrator meets Firpo here for
the first time; in *Sunday at Te Parenga*
he already knows him.

ONE SUNDAY MORNING, I AM EARLY ON THE BEACH AND MEET the sun showing a rim above the pale sea. The breeze off the water is damp and warm. I sniff its soft, salty breath: summer is in the air.

I find my way to the rocks, push my finger in the black, daisy-faces of the sea-anemones, watch the lazy ruffs of strings tremble, shiver, then with a swift embrace, close over my finger. A flash, a glitter in the pool—a shrimp hangs still near my finger—flash, it is gone. I grab a stick and stir the water to a cauldron, waiting for him to whirl out by centrifugal force, a silver cyclist on the Wall of Death, but he's hiding. I learned "centrifugal" yesterday.

I draw a heart in the sand with my toes, put my initials in it and then—after thought—another pair. Draw a long arrow through it, mark in the V-head with a firm, big toe. Give a grimace of disgust: race for the rocks.

I bound on to a broad terrace of rock, sloping up. Beside me, a bank of clay, striped like pyjamas in brown and yellow, dives and buries itself in the sand. A geological fault, my father tells me. I see a sad-eyed giant called Geology—in pyjamas—condemned for some Grievous Fault to live with his head in the sand for ever: this is his leg.

I clamber on and now the sea is far below me, swelling and gurgling in the fissured rock. Round the corner of the cliff with care because the root you swing round on is working loose and there, ahead, hanging right down the cliff, is the green staircase.

I have passed it a hundred times on my way to the king and queen at full tide; leaned on it, hung my towel on it, sat on the lowest step, seen no more than boards and planks, rusting nails and flaking green paint. But now, inexplicably, it is bathed in unholy light. It's the Beanstalk, and I am Jack and I know that I must go up, now, and explore the fabulous landscape at the top, find the castle, ask for food, trick the giantess, hide in the oven, steal the goose, kill the giant. I know the giant and giantess already: the Atkinsons, old and stinking rich. She's all right, tall and stringy with a head like a dandelion flower—I always want to blow on it and see her sparse grey hair fly off—but he's a white-haired, creaking wobbly wreck, always at Rotorua to soften up his brittle bones. Sometimes we see them on the beach in the evenings: the old man picks his way along with a stick and as you pass, you hear his old bones go click, click.

I fill my lungs with air and rush at the steps, patter up the cliff-face, sea, rocks, king and queen receding and diminishing below me, reach an old iron gate. Push and enter. Into the Giant's Demesne.

An old rock garden, writhing with weeds. A jungle of *raureka* and gorse, stabbing at my bare arms and legs. On and into a clearing and—there's the giant's castle, enormous and forbidding in white stonework. Take the lower path, down into a shallow gully, up again on to a flat piece scooped out of the cliff. And there, ringed in huge clumps of wild broom, a little house, an old bach, a tumbledown whare. I bang my head. I tingle.

Softly I step on to the porch. Boards are broken here and there; dirt and a mulch of soft leaves. Window, door. The window gapes at me, sightless, crossed boards nailed from the inside. Now for the door. Push, and a shuddering creak. Fearful, I look over my shoulder. Silence. Again and with a stifled, high-pitched whine of anguish, it yields and lets me in. Thick dust springs away from my feet in soft arcs.

An old tin chimney at the back, a few blackened twigs in the grate. A table and a battered chair, rimed with dust. A calendar

66

on the wall, five years old, a pretty Chinese girl on the cover, pink, sweet and glazed as a toffee apple. A scrap of newspaper on the floor. . . .

'Captain Dreyfus, Officer of the French Legion of Honour and victim of the most infamous political persecution in modern history, died last week. . .',

The wind stirs. Grudgingly, the door opens a little more. A band of light shoots through to the chimney, flaring on the blackened twigs in the grate. Particles of dust jostle, spin and dance in the light. The swelling pods of broom outside give a little dry shiver.

A swish of grass, a step on the porch. I rush to the door. I am staring at the thinnest man I have ever seen, dressed in dirty jeans and the top half of a tattered woollen bathing suit, button gone on the shoulder. The face. Long, whitish, with two bulbs of eyes that stare not at me but restlessly about, grey bristly hair, a mouth full of broken teeth.

"Gidday, boy. Who are you?"
I tell him my name. "Who are you?"
He shivers. His head flicks upwards.
"Firpo's the name."
"Firpo what?"
"Just . . . Firpo."
He stands frozen, as if his name, spoken, makes him the centre of a magic field. Then he grabs my shoulder, forces me in.
"Are you a good boy? A kind boy?"
I shrug, think a moment.
"Oh, yeh. Suppose so."
"How old are you?"
"Twelve and a bit."
He recoils from me, mutters darkly.
"Double figures. Don't like double figures."
"Why?"
"They laugh. Double figures laugh. Nine, seven, eight, six: they just look: they don't care. . . . Do you laugh much?"

67

What is he at? Uneasiness stirs in me.

"Oh, yeh. Quite a bit."

His eyes shift, look upwards.

"World's full of it. Ha ha ha. Ha ha ha. Takes your skin off. Leaves ya all bare. . . . Would you laugh at Firpo?"

I look at him closely, Is he loopy? The long white face, the eyes bulging, seeking shelter.

"No I don't think I would."

He stares at me a moment and his face softens. Then he turns away, seems to see the bach and its squalors for the first time. He lurches to the the table, bangs his hand on it: dust leaps upwards.

"She's sent me down here. Like an old dog."

"She has? Who?" I ask eagerly, sensing that the rough places will now be made plain. But he doesn't answer. He has seen the calendar on the wall, rushes to it and drags it down—the Chinese girl skims across the bach and disappears out the door. He takes a large piece of newspaper from his pocket and pushes it carefully over the nail. Suddenly he is all animation and excitement.

"Here, boy. C'm here. See? Cut it out yesterday. That's Jesse Cabot. Come to live at Te Parenga! Yeh, him. Heavyweight wrestling champ of the British Empire! Look at him, will ya? Look at that chest on him; look at those arms on him! One day, boy, I'll be like that. I'll wipe those smiles off. No more ha ha ha. Respect! Respect. Watch. Watch! Are you watching? On the hands, down!"

He buckles like a spring, his legs shoot out behind him, arms straight. He bends and unbends, trembling. Veins and ridges spring into his arms in livid welts, vanish, a shadow of blood behind them. A voice outside.

"Tim. Tim! Are you there, Tim?"

Firpo collapses, scrambles to his feet. One hand comes slowly forward, as if to repel something.

A thin elderly woman stands in the doorway, hair like an old mop, eyes mild but imploring: where have I seen this face before? Yes. It's the face of Firpo, transposed.

She advances. I recoil towards the chimney, my eyes on the thin froth of petticoat lace below her skirt.

"Well, Tim, Getting settled in? Not so bad, is it?" Her eye swivels, flicks open: me. "Bless my soul! Who's this?"

"Good morning, Mrs Atkinson," I say, nervously.

"Oh, you know me, do you." She comes closer, peers at me. "Yes, I know you, too. Live along the beach, don't you? That's right: I know your mother. What are you doing here?"

"Exploring, Mrs Atkinson."

"Exploring, are you?" She gives a tinny cackle. "Trespassing's the word, my lad. All right: just a minute." She turns away from me. "Tim, I've got the stretcher out. It's quite sound. Needs a dust, that's all. I'm giving you three blankets. That should be enough. Come and get them later, will you? And you, young man. You can do something for me. Pay for your exploring. Come up to the house, will you? Tim, I've brought you a broom. It's on the porch. Start sweeping the place out, will you?"

Firpo stands as if in trance, his face stone-white, no breath moving the thin rib-cage. Mrs Atkinson looks at him a moment, uneasy, then her eyes blink, her hands shake.

"Oh, Tim. Tim! Don't look at me like that, dear! It's all for the best. Really, it is. All for the best," and she moves slowly towards the door, suddenly turns there.

"And remember one thing, Tim. Wherever you are, big house or tiny bach, it doesn't matter: God watches over you wherever you are," and she goes out. I follow her and look back at Firpo. He seems to uncoil slowly: our eyes meet.

"Well, what are you staring at? You heard her, didn't you?"

"Why did she call you Tim?"

"Get out!"

"Is your name Tim?"

He explodes and lunges towards me. I run out, scared.

Mrs Atkinson stands by the gorse.

"I'm waiting, son. No, there's no path here. Hasn't been used for years. Not since my children were small. Stick close to me and you can share my track. All right? Quick march!"

She seems to swim ahead, pushing her way through waist-high gorse, her old hands clearing the thorns in a feeble breast-stroke; the bushes close behind us with a swish and a flash of yellow.

The house looms up, rough-cast walls gleaming white. We pass from wilderness to new country, tended and civilized, concrete paths, flowering borders, roses on long stems.

"Do you like my roses?" she asks with a coy pride. "Could your mother grow roses like that?"

"Dunno. She hasn't got time, eh."

A gravel path and two glass doors, opening on a porch. She calls me in. I blink through the light scored in parallels by the venetian blinds. The red stone floor chills my bare feet and I feel out of place.

There, in a wheelchair, sits Mr Atkinson, a great loose frame of bones, white-haired, white-suited, white-moustached, white tufts sprouting from ears as large as mussel shells. He seems to have been passed through fire, leaving this heap of fierce whiteness: a touch and he will crumble to ash.

"Who's this, Ella?"

His voice scrapes and rumbles, dragging a ball of phlegm.

Mrs Atkinson titters nervously.

"I found him in the bach, Guy. Said he was exploring. You know him, dear. Those nice people along the beach."

"Come here."

I approach him, slowly. His eyes, kauri-gum colour, a net of red veins dropped on them, pierce me.

"Hmmmph! Well, how's he taking it, Ella?"

"Tim? Oh, not bad, Guy. As well as can be expected."

"He should never have left that asylum!"

She opens her mouth, sighs; her lips tremble.

"Blood's thicker than water, Guy."

70

"Is it? Well, I've my own ideas on that one, too!" he says with a sudden sinister emphasis.

She makes a sudden quick flurried movement of her hands.

"Oh, Guy, . . . in front of . . . !" She turns to me swiftly.

"Now, listen, son. This man you met just now, it's poor Tim Barlow, my sister Jane's son. She died last year, you know. He— well, I'm afraid he's not all there. Thinks he's someone else all the time. Firpo, or some such name. Guy, who was Firpo again?"

The old man rumbles, shouts suddenly, incomprehensibly.

"All right, Guy, all right. Don't shout at me! It's bad for my. . . . Well, look, son. You're old enough to know. He's not like other people, you can see that. Needs looking after. He's been in an asylum but he talked of killing himself all the time so they asked me to look after him. Well, you see, we just can't have him in the house. He's dirty and upsets things. But he'll be quite all right in the bach while the warm weather's on. Thank goodness we didn't pull it down, Guy! I'll stock him up with tins, he likes pipis, he can grow his own vegetables. . . ."

"Keep him busy, Ella. That's the thing!"

"Well, he's a good gardener, Guy: one thing he seems to like. Now—" and her fingers suddenly waggled as if she were playing the piano then joined together in an arch—"we don't want people to know about him. You can see that, son. We're well-known people. You're not to tell anyone, understand? Not even your own people. Promise."

From behind her, a sepulchral rumble.

"Promise!"

"All right."

"And you won't come here again, will you?"

I shake my head. Her face clears; through the old flesh a timid frightened girl flashes suddenly.

"Good boy. Now here's the little thing you can do for me. I've got his breakfast ready. Would you take it down to him on your way home? Don't want to push through that nasty old gorse again. Do you like sweets? . . . Good." Her face crumples into a wavering smile. "See if I can find you one."

I am left alone with the old man. The stick rattles on the

71

floor. His face becomes one huge sneer.

"Firpo." His head rears, his mouth writhes. "God! God."

Mrs Atkinson appears, a tray in her hands: porridge, toast, a pot of tea, milk, sugar, cup. She gives it to me, fishes in her pocket.

"I did find a sweetie. Do boys still like paper toffees?" she asked, unwrapping it. "Yes, I thought they might. Open," she says coyly and pops it in my mouth. "Goodbye, son. Don't forget your promise."

I mumble, my jaws stuck; walk out of the house through the trim garden and into the wild gorse, no hands to ward off the thorns, pricking, pocking my bare arms and legs. My arms ache.

The bach. Firpo is on the porch, sweeping with a strange, slim elegance, making the long smooth strokes of a master cricketer coming out to meet the ball. "Takes a pride in his work," I note, passing him. He makes no sign of recognition: I might not be there. A pile of leaves, thick grey skeins of webs, the calendar and the Chinese girl, the news of the death of Captain Dreyfus, topple off the porch and on to the long glinting spears of grass.

I walk into the bach, plump the tray down on the table; feel the ache flood out of my arms. I stand at the door and call:

"Here's your breakfast, Mr Barlow."

He rears as if stung: his face puckers like a nut. He rushes into the bach and leaps towards me.

"Firpo. Firpo. Firpo!"

He holds the broom over his head, chases me round the table. "FIRP-PAAAAH!"

The name strangles and rattles in his throat. I rush out, bound heedless through the gorse, patter down the green staircase, rocks, sand, path, house.

"Where's the fire?" asks my father, gardening, leaning on his hoe amazed as I flash past him

"Where have you been, dear?" calls my mother from the bed-room.

"Round the rocks!" I gasp and rush to my room.

"Well, don't forget it's the children's song service. See that your shoes are clean."

Her voice reaches me muffled, face down on my bed, heaving.

        *   *   *

We stand in line in a pew, primped and gleaming. My father trumpets the responses and sings a loud descant in the hymns. We stand, sit, kneel, sit. The last hymn. Flip the pages. . . .

> *All things bright and beautiful.* . . . Firpo
> *All creatures great and small,*
> *All things wise and wonderful*
> *The Lord God made them all.* . . . Firpo too? . . .
>   *Amen.*

Mr Thirle faces us in his swelling surplice and cassock, moist and mellow. Two fingers rise in benediction. "The grace of our Lord Jesus Christ and the love of God be with you all, this day, and for evermore. . . .' *Firpo.* He ambles off to the vestry and the choir follow him in pairs, faces grave and inward, like sheep in ruffs. . . . *Firpo.*

The first swim of the year, gasping, shouting, diving through my father's legs, floating through the soft, green, shot-silk light, springing out like a rocket, tossing the spray from my hair. . . . *Firpo.*

The day ends, the sharp clear contours of Te Parenga, blurring, thickening, dying. A red light winking on Rangitoto's dark front. My father standing by me looking out to sea, a long swell running.

"Dad? Who was . . . Firpo?"

My father looks at me a moment, speculatively.

"Firpo. Firpo. . . . Oh, yes. He was a famous South American boxer, wasn't it? Now didn't he and Jack Dempsey. . . . Oh well, anyway, he was a great athlete. A world-beater."

The dark swell heaves and flexes into a huge muscle, a white rope of foam on its crest and dashes for the shore, spurting and hissing on the shingle.

*   *   *

Summer advances. The sand in the week-ends is too hot to walk on and people in bright bathing suits come down and sunbake all day long. We have Sunday morning beer parties on our lawn and sometimes we don't have lunch until half-past two. The jellyfish make their annual three-day visit when the sea is like a tapioca pudding and the beach in the mornings strewn with little glittering blobs that we throw about or drop down bathing suits. For a few days, a squadron of Portuguese men-of-war cruises into the shallows like evil submarines, puffed, mottled blue and purple, sinister ribbons trailing.

One Sunday, it's a scorcher. All the islands in the Gulf are turned up at the edges, like little boats. Yachts drift tiredly in the channel with slack sails. The beach swims with heat, in wavering pools. We've been on the beach since nine o'clock and now, at half-past eleven, we've had five swims. My parents, Auntie Kass and Uncle Jim are exchanging stories with their friends in low voices and barks of laughter tell me that another one has been successfully delivered. My brother is building a castle, moated, battlemented, crusted with shells. Over by our gate, Joe Dyer and Bob Ferguson, skylarking. They must be twenty-one or so, lean and body-proud. One lies on his back in the sand, knees bent, hands up; the other lightly vaults and presses palm to palm, legs slowly rising till erect. They hold the pose like figures in a copper frieze, collapse and try another.

The sun beats down, licking our flesh with a searing tongue. I am almost asleep.

"Look!"

I sit up. Crikey! There's Firpo, prancing along the beach like a mettlesome horse, his knees lifting rhythmically high in the air, still the old jeans and frayed bathing top—the loose strap bounces wildly on his chest. Behind him, a tribe of gleeful small boys, legs lifted high to keep in time. They advance along the beach like a grotesque dance troupe: Firpo, the ageing guest artist, aloof and haughty, the junior *corps de ballet* trying out its paces. A wave of laughter leaps up from the sprawling bodies on the sand.

"Who is it?"
"Where's he sprung from?"
"J'ever see such a rooster?"

My brother shouts "Coming?" and rushes off to join the mob. I tear off after him, giggling, and find myself face to face with Firpo, the long absorbed face, the shifting bulbs of eyes. He stops, looks at me, suddenly illumined.
"Gidday, boy!"
I look him up and down, coldly.
"Hello."
"Why haven't you been to see Firpo, eh?"
I think a moment.
"Trespassers will be prosecuted," I say in my small, cold way.
"Trespassers will be. . . . Oh! Away! They're away! Sick as a dog, he is! Gone to soak his old bones! Hope he rots!"
So they're away!
A bland voice at my side.
"Aha! Won't you introduce me to your friend?"
Uncle Jim, face solemn and beadily intent. I know that look. Uncle Jim is going to be a card.
Firpo swells, his face tightens.
"Firpo's the name. Firpo." As if he might say, "I am the Resurrection and the Life."
Uncle Jim pumps at his limp hand.
"Mr Firpo. Welcome to Te Parenga. Come and meet the folks. Come on, now! Don't be shy!"
He leads him towards our group. Firpo's step is springy, his eyes wide and darting. He stands before them, prim and erect.
"Now, folks. A big honour for us all. I want you to meet my

75

friend Mr Firpo. Kass dear: Mr Firpo. Bert: get up off your chuff and say hullo to a gentleman."

Firpo bows, suddenly courtly and elegant. Uncle Jim pilots him round the group of sedulously straight-faced sunbathers.

"And now, Mr Firpo," he continues, still in the same mocking, lofty style I have learned to dread, "we see you have begun training. May one ask what for?"

"One may," say Firpo graciously. "Firpo'll tell you. He's getting himself fit for the Olympic Games!"

A subdued gurgle from the sand, a muffled explosion of laughter. Uncle Jim quells it sternly.

"O yes,' he says, still bland and solemn, "and what events are you trying for?"

"Events? E—. Oh! All of them," Firpo says, with a lofty finality.

Uncle Jim squeezes his hand, thumps him on the back.

"Mr Firpo. On behalf of us all here at Te Parenga, may I say what an honour it is to have you with us. And we wish you wonderful, thumping good luck. Don't we?" he roars, whipping on the group. Smiles, vanish; the frieze of faces is expressionless. "Come on, now. Don't we!"

"Oh yes, yes, yes, yes!" they assure him solemnly, in chorus.

Firpo looks at them and his face breaks into a wavering smile.

"Wull, time presses. Yes, it presses. Firpo must be on his merry way! Cheerio, one and all."

He holds up his hand as if to stop traffic then whirls it round in a grotesque salute, his knees jerk into their piston movement and he prances off to his suite of small followers. They welcome him with shouts of joy. Off they trot, a flotilla in line ahead.

Pent-up seriousness collapses under a flood of laughter. Joe Dyer and Bob Ferguson roll in the sand, beating it with their fists, shouting.

"Jim, Jim, you were dreadful!" shrieks Auntie Kass. "Dreadful, dreadful, dreadful! I thought I'd bust!"

"By God, you're a dag, Jim," says someone admiringly.

"Well, I'll say this for the old beach," says Uncle Jim. "Never a dull moment with birds like that on it."

My mother looks after the retreating figures.

"Poor soul," she says suddenly, turning to her friends. "But they say people like that are very happy. . . ."

A single gull wheels overhead with a long harsh cry.

II

What was I to do about Firpo? He stuck in my mind like a piece of grit. Grimaced and postured there, absurd and touching. And there was something else when everyone was laughing at him. Dignified? Noble? No. Not at all. But something. Something. . . .

Yesterday, after tea, my father:

"That rooster on the beach today. Do you know him?"

"Aw no, Dad, I don't know him. Saw him once before, that's all."

"Well, be careful! Don't know what they're like. Might get into trouble. Watch yourself or before you know where you are. . . .'

My mother at the door.

"Telephone! Hurry, dear, a penny in the slot."

"Hello?"

77

A harsh grating voice strains through the grille.

"Aw, gidday, This is Joe Dyer. You know: on the beach yes'day. We're halfway up your street. Yeh: corner box. Could you meet me and Bob for a tick?"

"Now? What for?"

"We'll tell you when we see you, eh. We'll start walkin' down towards your gate, okay?" Click, and he is gone.

A minute passes. I slip out the front door and reach the gate. Two figures stand under the street lamp, faces smudged and hollowed. They look smaller than yesterday's bronzed animals, diminished, constricted.

"Hi. Now, listen. We saw you talkin' to that Firpo coot. D'you know where he lives?"

I hesitate.

"Why do you want to know?"

"Never mind. Do you?"

After a moment, I nod.

"Good on you. Thought you did. Would you take a letter to him?"

"Why can't you?"

"Aw, no. Better for you to, eh. You know him, see."

"What's it about?"

Their faces become wary, alert.

"Aw, no. That's private, eh. Just for him. Will you do it?"

He holds out a white envelope. I see on it, in type: *Mister Firpo: by hand*. That decides me. If it's typed and it says 'mister', it must be all right. I stretch out my hand: take it.

"All right. I'll take it after school, tomorrow."

They exchange glances.

"Good on you. Cheero."

They move out of the light and into the dark street. There is a sudden snorting noise like pigs rooting, then they dive off into the night.

Next day, after school, I make for the rocks, the envelope in my pocket, climb the stairs, pass through the gate. The gorse has been cut and the paths cleared. Down the gully, into the clearing and there's the bach, newly painted, gleaming green. The clumps

of broom have grown and the yellow flowers are out: the whole
bank is a wall of rich light. I step onto the porch, pass through
the door. The stretcher, loosely made, a pile of driftwood by the
old chimney, a long line of tins on the sheft, Jesse Cabot, squat
and glowering, still pinned to the wall. I stare at his image: body
flexed to show the lumps of muscle knotting out of the taut
flesh, bulging everywhere, inflated and rubbery, shining with
grease.

"Gidday, boy!"

Firpo on the porch, a hoe in his hand.

He moves in, comes towards me.

"So you did come to see Firpo, eh! How's tricks, boy! How's
tricks?"

He is all feverish animation: his face twitches with pleasure.

"Hello . . . Firpo."

It's the first time I've said his name. He responds at once. His
whole frame enlarges and grips around his title.

"Come to see how Firpo's gettin' on, diddun yer. Good on you,
boy! Good on you!"

I hold out the letter.

"This is for you, Firpo."

He stares at it, his eyes bulge.

"Mr Firpo: by hand," he mutters, grabs it, rips it open.

"Dear Mr Firpo. . . ."

He looks at me uncertainly, looks back at the paper, his eyes
close to the script.

"We hear you are a con—. . . we hear you are c-c-c. . . ."

He looks at me again, imploring, thrusts the letter at me.

"Boy. Boy! Read it, will ya?"

I take the letter from him, wondering: read.

"Dear Mr Firpo,

*We hear you are a contestant for the Olympic
Games. Some of our local boys have begun training too, and we
think it might be good practice for them if we had a friendly challenge race on the beach. The tide will be out next Saturday afternoon, and three o'clock should be a good time. The athletic club*

will provide a starter. The course will be along to the first cable post: no handicaps. So we hope to see you next Sunday afternoon at 3 o'clock.

(sgd) *Joe Dyer*
Bob Ferguson

"Firpo," I say gently, returning it to him, "are you going to do it?"

He stands rigid, frozen. A gust of breath wheezes through him. His face is molten.

"Yeh. Yeh! Firpo'll do it! He'll do it. . . ."

He stumbles a few steps, stands in front of the chimney, gazing at it as if it were a shrine, then turns back to me.

"Firpo's the name. Know that, don't ya. Wull, Firpo can do anything at all, see, anything you like to name. But what do they do to Firpo, eh? Yeh, what do they do? They shut him up; they hide him away from the sun; they give him another name. But it's Firpo, Firpo, always Firpo! The time's coming—ohohoho yes, it's not far away, when Firpo will have his day and what will he be then, boy? What will he be then?" His voice drops to a hoarse whisper: his face beside mine. "A made man. Did you hear me, boy? Shall I say it again? A made man. Made man! Made man! Made man!"

His voice cracks. He trembles and shivers. I feel in the presence of Revelation: the veil of the temple is rent from top to bottom. He stumbles back to the chimney, gazing at it as if it held the secret of his being. Mystery, awe.

"Firpo," I say gently. "Firpo." No answer. No recognition. I back away from him softly, close the door slowly on his rigid back. I am alone.

I reach the beach and march briskly along. A deep voice like the headmaster's on Friday morning parade begins rumbling in my head. *"Left, right, left, right"* . . . no. No, no, no. That's not what the voice is saying. *Made man, made man.* Yes! Made Man! A man half-finished, soon to be made whole. By—Him up there, Who can move mountains and from Whom no secrets are hid? No, no. By me. By me!

An extraordinary exhilaration runs over my limbs; my soul is full of The Made Man. I giggle, run, gallop. *"Made Man, Made Man,"* the voice patters away. I reach the house exhausted. *"Maaade Maan,"* the voice whispers on a long breath: leaves me alone.

Homework. Sums. *If a train, a hundred yards long, travelling at sixty miles an hour, passes another in fifteen seconds, also travelling at sixty miles an hour, how long. . . .* Firpo. The Made Man. Firpo at the Games. Firpo leading the field in the half-mile, Firpo floating across the pit in the long jump, Firpo's 'great thews' quivering as he puts all his weight behind the shot. Firpo on the dais, laurel leaves on his brow. The voice of Firpo. *"Thank you, thank you. I just want to tell you that I owe all my success to a fair-headed boy in far-away New Zealand who stood beside me when all was grey. Cheerio, one and all. . . ."* Oh, shut up, shut up! The noble figure of my imagination blacks out.
If a train travels. . .
If Firpo travels. . .

Wednesday.

Walking to school, a bus approaching. If I reach that telegraph pole before the bus, Firpo will win. I reach it, gasping. The four concrete steps into school. Take them in one bound and Firpo will win. I land, sprawl, graze my knee. I wear my bandage like an honourable wound, a service scar. Home again. If you chew forty bites to every mouthful, Firpo will win. Aching jaws. Mouth full of slimy pap.

"Eat up, dear!" calls my mother. "What's the matter with you? I want to clear away!"

Thursday.

Mr Stephen Irons comes from London; he is on a year's exchange in the 'Colonies.' Once a week, he does his best to inaugurate us into the glories of English literature. We loathe him, find him superior and edgy, throw darts and pass notes while he reads to us in a voice of honeyed weariness:

I wandered lonely as a cloud,
That floats on high o'er dales and hills,
When all at once, I saw a crowd,
A host of golden daffo. . . .

"Boy. Boy! What are you doing there?"

I look up, my face like a scrubbed cherub.

"Nothing, sir."

"Nothing, sir, nothing sir: you were drawing! I saw you. Bring it out here."

I take my piece of paper to his desk. His eyes flick wide apart behind his glasses. He sees a bulging gargoyle, immensely muscled, chest like the prow of a Spanish galleon, waist so fine a quick jerk would snap it.

"And what might this be?" he inquires ,with a chilling hauteur.

I hesitate, unwilling to expose my private ikon.

"Well?" he snaps at me.

"The Made Man, sir."

He rears, startled.

"The made man? The made man. I see. This thing, this— monster, is the summit of all human endeavour, is it?"

"I don't know what you mean, sir."

"Oh."

He shows it to the class.

"This is what your friend prefers to Wordsworth."

There is a dutiful cackle, but they are on my side. They *much* prefer it to Wordsworth. Mr Irons knows this. His face narrows and sharpens.

"Yes, you may well laugh."

He screws The Made Man into a ball, throws it on the floor.

"Now, listen to me, you boys. This cult of brawn over brains that you all go in for can lead a country to ruin. I don't need to remind you of what's happening in Germany: you can read the papers. I didn't think I'd find it here. After all, you're British! Or you were until a little while ago . . . Shakespeare, Milton, Wordsworth—all British! I didn't think the British would have rubbed off so soon. Young savages. . . ."

The young savages stare at him stolidly, blankly. He gives a sigh of defeat, turns back to me.

"All right, get back to your seat. You will write out for me a hundred times: the pen is mightier than the sword and brains will go farther than brawn."

He picks up the book, his air limp and dejected.

"Same place".

> *Beside the lake, beneath the trees,*
> *Fluttering and dancing, in the breeze. . . .*

Friday.

My father in the bathroom, shaving.

"Dad? How do you put on weight and get big muscles?"

My father ponders, looks at me critically, dips his brush and lathers his cheek.

"Well yes, you do look a bit on the weedy side, old chap. Do ten push-ups every morning. Give you arms like a blacksmith."

I giggle at his mistake.

"No, no, Dad. It's not for me. For someone else. He does push-ups already."

My father draws the razor down his face. A canal of pink flesh appears between banks of soap.

"Oh. Well, diet's important. Plenty of meat, body-building substance. Steak, chops, liver. All that."

I recoil. Steak, chops, liver! But Firpo lives on pipis, tea, bread and jam! I rush to my money-box. Fifteen and fourpence. I leave the fourpence, take the fifteen shillings to the butcher's after school.

"How much can I get for this?"

The butcher screws his face up, looks at me curiously, wipes bloodied hands on his apron.

"Oh! Your Mum run out of ideas, eh? All right: let her try this for size," and he unhooks a huge joint from the line of carcasses behind him. I stumble out, carrying half a sheep, stagger to the rocks, totter up the steps and arrive gasping at the bach.

Firpo is on the porch, shelling pipis into a pot.

"Firpo, look! Look what I've brought you!"

Firpo rises, looks, unwraps it wonderingly, gives a grimace of disgust.

"What's this for, boy?"

"For you! To build your body up for Sunday!"

Firpo shakes his head slowly.

"Aw, no. No, no, no. Don't eat meat, boy. Cruel, killing things. Vegetarian, Firpo is.'

"Aw, Firpo, don't be silly!" I shout at him, in exasperation. "What about those pipis?"

His face takes on an air of scholarly, academic cunning as of a philosopher sifting categories.

"Oh, that's different, boy. You see—pipis, they can't feel, they don't know. But animals, they feel. They—know."

"But—how are you going to build your body up for Sunday."

Firpo expands and beats his chest.

"Fit! Fit! Fit as a fighting tomcat, Firpo is!"

He performs a little jig, feinting grotesquely on the air. I give up.

"But—Firpo! What am I going to do with this?"

He stops; allows the thought to settle.

"Aw, I dunno, boy. Take it home to your Mum, eh."

I stand irresolute, then rage suddenly chokes me.

"Silly fool!" I scream, grab the joint and rush off, tears of fury in my eyes, the Hunter returned from the Kill.

I stamp into the kitchen, throw the carcass on the table.

"Mum. Mum! Here's a joint for you."

My mother, at the stove turns, aghast.

"But I've got a joint, dear! It's in the oven."

"Oh, well." I giggle foolishly. "Here's another."

My mother advances, amazed.

"But where did you get it?"

"Butcher's!" I say in a lofty rasp, as if she needed her head read.

"What with, may I ask?"

"Pocket money."

"How much?"

"Fifteen bob," I say, swallowing.

My mother rushes to the joint and lifts it up, straddling it across her arms.

"Fifteen bob! He was robbing you. All your pocket money. But dear—what's it for?"

"Present!" I shout, suddenly inspired.

She looks at me closely—does she see that I am close to tears?

"Well, thank you, dear. How very sweet of you," she says wonderingly. "This'll last a week! How am I going to keep it?"

"I don't know!"

I rush to my room, unable to say another word, beat my pillow in a frenzy of rage. Later, I hear my father say:

"What an extraordinary thing! Do you think the boy's gone a bit loopy? Er . . . any insanity in your family, dear? . . ."

So Friday goes.

Saturday afternoon.

One hope left. One last hope. I say I'm going for a walk, pass along the beach, up the Strand, round the corner to the Church. It shakes with sound as I approach, the organ in beefy roars, the shrill screams of women being put through a mangle, the buzz of singing men. Choir practice. I grope in the sudden gloom and there's the choir: eight ladies and—two men, Mr Thirle in front, waving his hands. They roar away, biting the air in quick, toothy gulps or hold their mouths open on a long note: you could throw a ping-pong ball in them. I find a pew at the back, pull down the hassock, kneel, clasp my hands.

"Listen, God, listen. I want to talk to you about a man called Firpo. . . ."

"Praise Him! Praise Him! Praise Him! Praise Him!"

"Listen God. . . ."

"Praise Him! Praise Him!"

The singing goes on, solid waves of sound, pulsing, throbbing. *Praise Him.* How can God listen to that muck? He must be deaf already. Mr Thirle claps his hands. A sudden hush.

"Oh now, that's a minim you've got there, Miss Mackay. Not

a crotchet. Two beats, not one. Two, two, two. Not one. Don't forget it, now."

I rush in, my eyes closed.

"Listen, God, listen! You've got to make Firpo win. Did you hear me? Firpo, Firpo, Firpo. Firpo must win. Firpo."

"All right, choir, letter B. Bottom of page. And remember: it's a song of praise—not a funeral dirge. One, two!" and the sound rushes into the empty air, filling every space. *Ally loo yah, ally loo yah* roar the men; *loo yah! loo yah! loo yah!* scream the women, like a herd of cows, lowing to be milked, screeched over by maddened cowgirls. I fidget, bite my nails. God wants time to think this over. Time is running out! Stop that racket, stop, stop, stop.

"Shut up, for Christ's sake!" I yell, frenzied.

Complete silence.

The organ expires on a little wheezing thread, mumbles with shock. Mr Thirle slowly turns, shading his eyes.

"Who's there?"

I stand up.

"It's me, Mr Thirle."

He comes towards me, grave and ominous.

"And what are you doing here, lad?"

"Praying!" I rasp out at him.

His face contracts, looks graver still.

"Done something wrong, lad? Asking for forgiveness?"

"No. I was just praying for summing to happen."

"Hmm. Well, it's no call to take the Lord's name in vain in His own house, is it lad? God doesn't like that kind of talk. You'll put Him off. He won't listen."

"Oh won't he?" I ask, in panic.

"No, He won't! You come to Him with respect. You don't profane His house!"

"But you were all making so much noise, he couldn't hear me!" I shout, despairing.

Mr Thirle recoils, shocked.

"What's that? So much noise? A *Magnificat* of my own composition, in four parts? Choir: did you hear that? You've got a critic here, it seems."

A rustle of indignation: Mr Thirle holds up his hand, quells it, turns back to me severely.

"Now, listen to me, my lad. If you'd kept a civil tongue in your head, I might have been prepared to listen. But I don't like cheeky boys. You get along home."

"Can't I come back when you've finished?"

"No, you can't!" he thunders. "I won't have you in my Church in that frame of mind. I'll be speaking to your parents about this. On your way."

His eyes, stern and focussed with indignation, follow me out.

I reach the hard sand. Tomorrow it will carry Firpo; the sand will be pocked and dented with his 'flying feet'. Oh, if only the day would freeze and stop, the sun be fixed for ever, the night and morning never come.

Firpo's on his own, now. God's deaf, and Firpo's on his own, I feel tense and full of dread.

III

Sunday comes, a white mist at dawn, a yellow haze at noon. God's deaf, all right. I spend the morning, nervous and feverish. At a quarter to three, I go on to the porch and look along the beach. A large clot of people has gathered and I can see several young men in shorts and singlets, bouncing up and down.

I rush down the path to the beach. The tide is out, the sand firm, the weather pitilessly fine.

Before I reach the chattering group by the rocks, I see that Firpo is not there. My heart gives a sudden bound. Firpo has forgotten. Firpo has fallen through the steps and shattered on the rocks. Firpo is dead. There I stand by the grave, the solitary mourner, watching the simple coffin slowly, slowly sink. Earth to earth, ashes to—the rocks. And there's—crikey, what's he doing here—Sergeant Robinson, the starter, holding a sawn-off pistol which he is throwing up and catching in an irritable kind of way and there are the contestants, six of them, hopping about, spreading their arms and throwing them about their bodies, turning their trunks in jerks from one side to the other. I mingle with the crowd and at once seem part of their talk.

"Is he any good?"
"Olympic Games: he's hopeful."
"Who does he think he is, anyway?"
"Half a moll, iddunut?"
"Give ya bob on young Ferguson here."

The talking dies suddenly to a low, tense buzz. Round the rocks comes Firpo, dressed as always in his dirty jeans and frayed bathing top, tattered canvas shoes. Round his shoulders, an old vari-coloured tweed coat. He takes in the group with a single glance, his eyes set, his air portentous and formidable, then raises his hand in greeting. There is a murmur of discomfort, and Sergeant Robinson calls out:
"Come on, Samson, or whatever your name is. We're all waiting for you."
Firpo does not hurry his dignified, measured gait. He arrives, shakes hands with each of the contestants gravely and begins a sort of hopping dance. One leg flashes up: he touches it casually with his index finger. A final whirl of his arms and he is ready.

He removes his coat and pants to reveal the lower half of his bathing suit. The crowd has been respectful up till now: Firpo's self-possession has carried a weird authority. But the sight of those wicker-basket arms and legs beside the muscled calves and biceps of his opponents, is too much. There is a titter, then laughter. "This is gunna be good," says one, stifling snorts. The athletes move away from him with significant smiles, each one reflecting: "Yeh, well I can't be last now."

The crowd has become one in its humour and has begun to barrack.

"Come on, Ted: we're watching you, boy."

"Give it to 'em, Joe. Got nothin' to lose."

Oh, hasn't he, hasn't he just, I think, a raging vapour rising in me.

"Come on, Firpo!" I yell and then, as the crowd focusses on me, I grow red and ashamed and wish the sand would cover me up.

"That kid's his pet," says a man beside me, rolling a cigarette disdainfully.

"I am not!" I shout, sensing deep insult. "Don't you dare—"

"All right, break it up, break it up!" shouts Sergeant Robinson. "Okay, boys, you can get ready." And with this, we fall silent, forget everything else.

Robbie turns to us.

"Now listen you folk. I got a pretty good idea why you invited me down here. Well, that's not my business. But you're not gunna make a Joe Hunt outa me, get it? You want a race, all right. It's gunna be run properly. Just so long as that's clear".

He turns to the runners.

"Now, boys. You're not to break. You wait for the gun. That's all you have to do: wait for the gun. Your course is along to the first cable. The judges are there now."

He waves a white handkerchief: far along the beach, another flutters.

"All right, then. On your marks."

He raises the gun and the seven men crouch down on their line of pipi shells, Firpo in the middle, three on each side of him.

He looks like an old hawk, squatting there.

"Get set!"

Seven behinds move slowly upwards. We all seem to take the same breath, then let it out with a gasp. One of the runners has fallen forward, trots a few paces. Robbie brings the gun down, spins it round his thumb. His face reflects a deep, deep sorrow.

"Can't you boys get it? Not all that difficult, is it? Wait for the gun! Here, young lad. Don't you understand English? Wait, wait, wait for the gun! Now look at Samson there. He hasn't moved."

It was true. All the others had jumped up and were dancing around, arms and legs flopping loosely like rag dolls, but Firpo doesn't move. He stays kneeling in the sand, inward, rigid, tense, waiting. It's impressive. A slight uneasiness runs through the crowd.

"Wonder if he's any good?" says someone, softly.

Down they go again. On your marks. Get set. With my eyes on the back of Firpo's head, I think the bang will never come. When it does, I hardly hear it. Because Firpo has left the mark as if propelled by a giant boot: already he is ahead. I feel a shiver run right down my spine. Firpo is moving forward in great loping bounds: he seems to touch the sand with regret, his arms hardly move. Behind him, the six young men in a pack, arms and legs pumping frantically, like puppies following a horse.

The crowd is silent.

"By Christ, he can run though, can't he?" someone mutters at last. "Not such a young joker, either."

I find my voice. No fear of rebuff now.

"Come on Firpo! Oh, you beauteeee!"

They are about seventy-five yards off. Firpo is still ahead, but— and as if to answer the doubt in my mind, a voice behind me says, "Aw, he'll never keep this up. They're gaining on him already." Firpo and the pack have become one jiggling clot from which his head leaps up, like a porpoise, springing for air. And now, with the quiet despair that follows unreasonable joy, I see the pack divide round Firpo and leave him exposed like a rock before the receding tide. Firpo gives one desperate wild lunge into the air after them, and falling heavily like a gawky albatross, lies on the sand, still.

There is a great shout of laughter. It is a comedy after all: the funny scene has just come later than usual. "God, what a nut! Olympic Games! Oughta be locked up!" I could feel relief in their laughter: the Comic Muse had done her stuff and they would not have to cope with a Firpo who had won. "And will you look at young Joe Dyer there! Come on, boy! Win me my bob! Ya got 'em all beat." Yes, now they could enjoy the race.

After the first chilling shock, I grab Firpo's coat and pants and run. He lies flat, right in front of our gate. I can see my parents at the window: will they be angry? Then Firpo abruptly arches his back and is shaken by a long fit of dry retching. He kneels there, groaning, shaking his head back and forth, then he sees me. He looks at me with clear eyes, suddenly mild and full of comprehension.

"I'm done, boy. Done." He puts out his hand. "Will you help me up, boy?"

I drape the coat round the thin shoulders, slowly raise him to his feet. His face is sand-grey and the rim of dark stubble on his cheeks looks stuck on, like the fur on a mussel shell. He staggers a few steps, gives a wheezing cough.

"Here, Firpo. Don't get cold. Put on your pants, eh."

He clambers into them awkwardly, leaning on me. I feel a sudden sharp warmth. I've never been so happy in my life.

We move slowly along the beach, and Firpo seems to revive a little. The race is over and the crowd has straggled. Joe Dyer has won and a few moments later the runners come trotting back for their coats. They pass us and shrug, gallop on, stop. Joe Dyer talks with them a moment, leaves them and comes trotting back to us. He looks at Firpo, troubled. Firpo stands dejected, head down, refusing to meet his eye.

"Look, ah. Ah. You know—it was only a joke, you know. Meant no harm. Just for a bit of fun."

Firpo gives no sign of having heard him. Joe Dyer looks at him again, trying to gauge the depth of his suffering.

"Well, anyway, best man won, diddun he? See ya 'round!" and he gallops off.

We move on, on, passing through lines of people. They watch us, sniggering and silent until we have passed then turn to stare, tapping their foreheads or whirling their hands beside their ears until we are at the rocks, alone.

Slowly we climb to the bach. I open the door, lead Firpo to the stretcher, pull the blankets about to some semblance of comfort. Firpo sits on his bed and with the laboured deliberation of an old man, tries to take off his shoes.

"Here Firpo let me", I say flushed and happy to have him wholly dependent. I pull the laces, gently ease the shoes from his feet.

"Lie down, Firpo. Go on. You'll feel better then."

He looks at me a moment then throws himself face down on the bed, shoulders heaving. A thick muffled sound tells me that he is crying. Horrified, I fall on my knees beside the bed

"Oh, don't Firpo, don't. Look—" I sought wildly for some straw of comfort— "it was because you didn't eat that meat and build your body up. You can't win races if you don't build your body up. You've got to have muscle-power. You've got to."

Firpo turns his head. His face is streaked where the tears have run over the dirty flesh and there are bright beads on some of the bristles.

"No, no! Firpo's finished. That's the end of the made man! He's finished! Done, done, done.'

"And Firpo, look," I rushed on, "I prayed to God for you, but there was so much noise in the Church, he couldn't hear me, But next time I'll go when it's quiet and then He'll hear me, and then he'll help you, Firpo. . . .'

Firpo stiffens: his whole frame tightens.

"God. God. Did you say, God?"

With a lunge, his huge despair seems to explode.

"There's no God! No God! It's all a cheat, a cheat! How could there be. . . ." His voice trails into silence and he looks at me, his face suddenly sharp and malevolent.

"Get out. Get out! You've only come to laugh at Firpo, like all the others!"

I recoil, amazed, shattered.

"No, Firpo!"

"Get out!"

He seizes one of his shoes, hurls it at me. It strikes me on the cheek. I gasp with pain, stagger.

"Get out! Never come here again!"

And he grabs the other shoe, raises his arm.

I rush out, terrified, hurtle up the path, patter down the steps and reach the beach, heaving.

The day is peerless, glittering. The sand is a mat of yellow crystal and Rangitoto seems cradled in unmortal light, the dark blue sheet at its edge fading to the washed blue above. I feel drenched in its intolerable purity.

I stumble up the path to our house and there's my brother, sitting on the porch. He looks up at me, shyly.

"Gidday," he says, softly.

I give a gasping heave.

"Hello."

"We saw the race. From the v'randah. All of us."

"Yeh. I know."

"Hard cheese, eh."

I nod dumbly, surprised and touched at his insight.

"Are they angry? Mum and Dad?"

"Angry? Aw, no. Don't think so. Look: you know what? Mum's made some fruit salad for us and she sent me up the shops for ice cream." He looks up at me, uncertainly. "Um. You can have mine if you like."

I stand silent, unable to speak.

"Well, come on! What are you crying for, stupid? It's all ready. Let's go and have it, eh."

We move into the house together.

Christmas comes and goes, abundant and distending season. January moves on and soon the holidays left have to be counted on the fingers of two hands, then on one, and I am back at my desk as if I had never left it. The days shorten, slowly at first, then with a rush; the pohutukawa flowers sag and drop away, the hard clear light of summer yellows and wavers; there is more and more sand between the bathers on the beach.

One day, when the water is already chilling and one quick swim is enough, I find myself at the foot of the green staircase. A sudden impulse takes me to the top.

The paths are once more tangled and overgrown. Down the gully, into the clearing and there—the bach is gone. Well, not quite gone. A heap of rotting timber lies stacked up and there's the old tin chimney on one side, gaping.

A man sits on the porch, smoking. He looks up as I approach.

"Gidday, son."

"Hullo. You taking all this stuff away?"

"Yeh. That's right."

He takes a long pull on his cigarette.

"Where's Firpo?"

"Who?"

"Firpo. The man who lived here."

"Aw, the nutty joker? The athalete, you mean?"

I nod.

"Why: he a friend of yours?"

"I just know him, I wanted to see him."

"Aw, you wanted to see him, did you?" He gives a throaty chuckle. "Yeh, well you can too. Tuesdays and Thursdays, two to four." I look blank, uncomprehending. "Son, they've taken him off to the nuthouse. He was gettin' violent, you know. Took to old Mr Atkinson and you could hear right down the beach what he was sayin' 'bout Mrs Atkinson, who's been so good to him. So they carted him off in a straitjacket. Aw, weeks ago now."

He takes another pull; a thread of silver-blue smoke spirals upwards. He looks at me. "What's up, son? You feeling a bit crook?" He looks at me again, his eyes narrowing. "Look son. You gotta lock 'em up. Otherwise we'd all go loopy. He'll be all right. They'll look after him there. Give him everything he wants. He'll be happy now."

He stands up, rubs his frayed cigarette butt into the ground.
"Well, must be off. Should be through this job tomorrow. You gunna be around for a while?"
"Just for a minute."
"Well, don't you get into any mischief. Don't touch anything. I know what you boys are like. So long, son."

And shouldering a light pack, he passes through the bushes of broom. They close behind him with a little dry shiver.

I stand by the porch. The broom is almost bare of flowers,
and, as I watch, a jaundiced bloom flutters off the
bush, and sustained by the light breeze,
charts a hazy course before coming
to rest beside me. I pick it up
and somehow I know, as I
finger the jaded
petals, that
summer is
quite
at an
end